JOHN F. KENNEDY
TALKS TO
YOUNG PEOPLE

JOHN F. KENNEDY
TALKS TO
YOUNG PEOPLE

**Compiled and Edited by
NICHOLAS SCHNEIDER and
NATHALIE S. ROCKHILL**

HAWTHORN BOOKS, INC.

Publishers   New York

PHOTO CREDITS

page 41 by John Rees from Black Star
page 107 by Maude Cooke from National Audubon Society
all others from Wide World

1655

CONTENTS

FOREWORD

●

John F. Kennedy was an exceptional hero to young Americans. His youth and his dynamic optimism created a climate of positiveness, a certainty that no matter how great world problems are, they can be faced and dealt with successfully. His leadership is sorely missed. But the ideas that excited and inspired America while he was alive—of the untold possibilities for peace and prosperity that can and must be achieved, about the role the United States must play in world affairs, and about the unique contributions every person in the country can make—live on in President Kennedy's speeches and writing.

This collection of the President's words is presented in the belief that it will help young people to answer for themselves the challenge put forth in his inaugural address: "Ask what you can do for your country."

JOHN F. KENNEDY
TALKS TO
YOUNG PEOPLE

THE INAUGURAL ADDRESS

●

President John F. Kennedy's inauguration ushered in more than just another administration. As he took the oath of office in Washington on January 20, 1961, the watching world knew that a new era had begun, an era of youth, confidence, and dedication to America's ideals. The new President's inaugural address pointed out the path he intended to follow—and challenged America and the world to travel it with him:

We observe today not a victory of party but a celebration of freedom—symbolizing an end as well as a beginning, signifying renewal as well as change. For I have sworn before you and Almighty God the same solemn oath our forebears prescribed nearly a century and a half ago.

The world is very different now. For man holds in his mortal hands the power to abolish all forms of human poverty and all forms of human life. And yet the same revolutionary beliefs for which our forebears fought are still at issue around the globe—the belief that the rights of man come not from the generosity of the state but from the hand of God.

We dare not forget today that we are the heirs of that first revolution. Let the word go forth from this time and place, to friend and foe alike, that the torch has been passed to a new generation of Americans—born in this century, tempered by war, disciplined by a hard and bitter peace, proud of our ancient heritage—and unwilling to witness or permit the undoing of those human rights to which this nation has always been committed, and to which we are committed today at home and around the world.

Let every nation know, whether it wishes us well or ill, that we shall pay any price, bear any burden, meet any hardship, support any friend, oppose any foe to assure the survival and the success of liberty.

This much we pledge—and more.

To those old allies whose cultural and spiritual origins we share, we pledge the loyalty of faithful friends. United, there is little we cannot do in a host of cooperative ventures.

12

Divided, there is little we can do, for we dare not meet a powerful challenge at odds and split asunder.

To those new states whom we welcome to the ranks of the free, we pledge our word that one form of colonial control shall not have passed away merely to ·be replaced by a far more iron tyranny. We shall not always expect to find them supporting our view. But we shall always hope to find them strongly supporting their own freedom, and to rember that, in the past, those who foolishly sought power by riding the back of the tiger ended up inside.

To those peoples in the huts and villages of half the globe struggling to break the bonds of mass misery, we pledge our best efforts to help them help themselves, for whatever period is required—not because the Communists may be doing it, not because we seek their votes, but because it is right. If a free society cannot help the many who are poor, it cannot save the few who are rich.

To our sister republics south of our border, we offer a special pledge—to convert our good words into good deeds, to assist free men and free governments in casting off the chains of poverty. But this peaceful revolution of hope cannot become the prey of hostile powers. Let all our neighbors know that we shall join with them to oppose aggression or subversion anywhere in the Americas. And let every other power know that this hemisphere intends to remain the master of its own house.

To that world assembly of sovereign states, the United Nations, our last best hope in an age where the instruments of war have far outpaced the instruments of peace, we renew our pledge of support—to prevent it from becoming merely a forum for invective, to strengthen its shield of the new and the weak, and to enlarge the area in which its writ may run.

13

Finally, to those nations who would make themselves our adversary, we offer not a pledge but a request: that both sides begin anew the quest for peace, before the dark powers of destruction unleashed by science engulf all humanity in planned or accidental self-destruction.

We dare not tempt them with weakness. For only when our arms are sufficient beyond doubt can we be certain beyond doubt that they will never be employed.

But neither can two great and powerful groups of nations take comfort from our present course—both sides overburdened by the cost of modern weapons, both rightly alarmed at the steady spread of the deadly atom, yet both racing to alter that uncertain balance of terror that stays the hand of mankind's final war.

So let us begin anew—remembering on both sides that civility is not a sign of weakness, and sincerity is always subject to proof. Let us never negotiate out of fear. But let us never fear to negotiate.

Let both sides explore what problems unite us instead of belaboring those problems which divide us.

Let both sides, for the first time, formulate serious and precise proposals for the inspection and control of arms— and bring the absolute power to destroy other nations under the absolute power of all nations.

Let both sides seek to invoke the wonders of science instead of its terrors. Together let us explore the stars, conquer the deserts, eradicate disease, tap the ocean depths, and encourage the arts and commerce.

Let both sides unite to heed in all corners of the earth the command of Isaiah—to "undo the heavy burdens . . . [and] let the oppressed go free."

And if a beachhead of cooperation may push back the jungle of suspicion, let both sides join in creating a new endeavor, not a new balance of power, but a new world of

14

law, where the strong are just, the weak secure, and the peace preserved.

All this will not be finished in the first one hundred days. Nor will it be finished in the first one thousand days, nor in the life of this administration, nor even perhaps in our lifetime on this planet. But let us begin.

In your hands, my fellow citizens, more than mine, will rest the final success or failure of our course. Since this country was founded, each generation of Americans has been summoned to give testimony to its national loyalty. The graves of young Americans who answered the call to service surround the globe.

Now the trumpet summons us again—not as a call to bear arms, though arms we need—not as a call to battle, though embattled we are—but a call to bear the burden of a long twilight struggle, year in and year out, "rejoicing in hope, patient in tribulation"—a struggle against the common enemies of man: tyranny, poverty, disease, and war itself.

Can we forge against these enemies a grand and global alliance, North and South, East and West, that can assure a more fruitful life for all mankind? Will you join in that historic effort?

In the long history of the world, only a few generations have been granted the role of defending freedom in its hour of maximum danger. I do not shrink from this responsibility —I welcome it. I do not believe that any of us would exchange places with any other people or any other generation. The energy, the faith, the devotion which we bring to this endeavor will light our country and all those who serve it— and the glow from that fire can truly light the world.

And so, my fellow Americans: ask not what your country can do for you—ask what you can do for your country.

My fellow citizens of the world: ask not what America

15

will do for you, but what together we can do for the freedom of man.

Finally, whether you are citizens of America or citizens of the world, ask of us here the same high standards of strength and sacrifice which we ask of you. With a good conscience our only sure reward, with history the final judge of our deeds, let us go forth to lead the land we love, asking His blessing and His help, but knowing that here on earth God's work must truly be our own.

EDUCATION

●

President Kennedy spent more time on education, and made more speeches about it, than on any other domestic issue. According to his adviser Theodore Sorensen, it was the issue that mattered most to him. In today's increasingly complex world

—where everybody needs education to get a job, to contribute to the economy, to contribute as a citizen—too many people are getting too little education.

Kennedy urged young people to stay in school, to get as much education as they could. And he stressed time and time again that every educated person has the responsibility of contributing not just to his own financial well-being but to the community. Kennedy developed a reputation for an "intellectual" administration by surrounding himself with such scholars as Dean Rusk, former Rhodes scholar and one-time political science professor; and staff associates Arthur Schlesinger, a Harvard historian, and Walt Rostow of the Massachusetts Institute of Technology. Clearly the President put a premium on highly trained minds.

President Kennedy did everything he could to make more and better education available to all, both by presenting bills for aid to education and by using funds available to him as President. One important achievement of his administration was the Higher Education Act of 1963, which provided federal aid for colleges, additional classrooms, new community colleges, graduate centers, and better college libraries. He also broadened the reach of student loans and scholarships, and provided more funds for school lunches and libraries.

Kennedy, himself a *magna cum laude* graduate of Harvard College, knew very well the value of a trained mind in tackling any problem that presents itself. He wanted everyone to have that same advantage. Some of his thoughts on education, and on the educated citizen, follow:

Labor Day Message to the Youth of the Nation, September 3, 1962

I have an important message to deliver on this Labor Day to the youth of the nation.

My urgent message to you is, "Return to school."

For thousands of you, the decision you make this September about returning to school may mean the difference between possible hardship and unemployment or a fruitful life as a productive member of our society. . . .

Do not let yourselves be lulled into a false sense of security. If you have not completely availed yourselves of existing educational opportunities, and if you have not reached the full extent of your educational potential, do not make the mistake of not returning to school.

My Committee on Youth Employment has recently pointed out again that today a million young people, twenty-five and under, are out of school and out of work. Many of these youth are out of work because they do not have the educational background or training necessary to fit them into today's work force.

We know that 5 million jobs will open up in this decade for skilled workers, and yet, at the present time, the number of youth being trained for these jobs is totally inadequate.

In light of our national need for a better-prepared work force, it is tragic indeed to be reminded of the estimate that seven and a half million boys and girls will fail to complete high school during the decade of the 1960's, unless we, as a nation, take positive steps to prevent it. This situation is tragic, not only because it represents a great loss to our society in undeveloped talent and potential, but also because the outlook for these young people is black indeed.

There is no doubt that anyone without a high school diploma has a hard time finding a job today, and will have an even harder time in the years ahead, as jobs require an even higher degree of skill and training to perform. . . .

To you, the young people who have not completed your education—who may have dropped out of school—and to those who are considering doing so—go back to your school

19

desks when your school term begins. Go back with a real desire to learn. Go back with an intent and purpose that will make you a better student. Go back and become prepared, so when your time comes to enter the labor force, you will be a more valuable asset to our nation.

Special Message to the Congress on Education, January 29, 1963

In the new age of science and space, improved education is essential to give new meaning to our national purpose and power. In the last twenty years, mankind has acquired more scientific information than in all of previous history. Ninety percent of all the scientists that ever lived are alive and working today. Vast stretches of the unknown are being explored every day for military, medical, commercial, and other reasons. And finally, the twisting course of the cold war requires a citizenry that understands our principles and problems. It requires skilled manpower and brainpower to match the power of totalitarian discipline. It requires a scientific effort which demonstrates the superiority of freedom. And it requires an electorate in every state with sufficiently broad horizons and sufficient maturity of judgment to guide this nation safely through whatever lies ahead.

In short, from every point of view, education is of paramount concern to the national interest as well as to each individual. Today we need a new standard of excellence in education, matched by the fullest possible access to educational opportunities, enabling each citizen to develop his talents to the maximum possible extent.

Address at the University of North Carolina, October 12, 1961

I want to emphasize, in the great concentration which we now place upon scientists and engineers, how much we still need the men and women educated in the liberal traditions, willing to take the long look, undisturbed by prejudices and slogans of the moment, who attempt to make an honest judgment on difficult events. . . . I hope that you will realize that from the beginning of this country there has been the closest link between educated men and women and politics and government. And also to remember that our nation's first great leaders were also our first great scholars.

A contemporary described Thomas Jefferson as "a gentleman of thirty-two who could calculate an eclipse, survey an estate, tie an artery, plan an edifice, try a cause, break a horse, dance the minuet, and play the violin." John Quincy Adams, after being summarily dismissed by the Massachusetts legislature from the United States Senate for supporting Thomas Jefferson, could then become Boylston Professor of Rhetoric and Oratory at Harvard University, and then become a great Secretary of State.

And Senator Daniel Webster could stroll down the corridors of the Congress a few steps, after making some of the greatest speeches in the history of this country, and dominate the Supreme Court as the foremost lawyer of his day.

This versatility, this vitality, this intellectual energy, put to the service of our country, represents our great resource in these difficult days.

I would urge you, therefore, regardless of your speciality, and regardless of your chosen field or occupation, and regardless of whether you bear office or not, that you recog-

21

nize the contribution which you can make as educated men and women to intellectual and political leadership in these difficult days, when the problems are infinitely more complicated and come with increasing speed, with increasing significance, in our lives than they were a century ago when so many gifted men dominated our political life. The United States Senate had more able men serving it, from the period of 1830 to 1850, than probably any time in our history, and yet they dealt with three or four problems which they had dealt with for over a generation.

Now they come day by day, from all parts of the world. Even the experts find themselves confused, and therefore in a free society such as this, where the people must make an educated judgment, they depend upon those of you who have had the advantages of the scholar's education.

I ask you to give to the service of our country the critical faculties which society has helped develop in you here. I ask you to decide whether you will give the United States, in which you were reared and educated, the broadest possible benefits of that education.

It's not enough to lend your talents to deploring present solutions. Most educated men and women on occasion prefer to discuss what is wrong, rather than to suggest alternative courses of action. But, "would you have counted him a friend of ancient Greece," as George William Curtis asked a body of educators a century ago, "would you have counted him a friend of ancient Greece who quietly discussed the theory of patriotism on that hot summer day through whose hopeless and immortal hours Leonidas and the three hundred stood at Thermopylae for liberty? Was John Milton to conjugate Greek verbs in his library when the liberty of Englishmen was imperiled?" . . .

"A university," said Professor Woodrow Wilson, "should be an organ of memory for the state, for the transmission of its best traditions." And Prince Bismarck was even more specific. "One third of the students of German universities," he once said, "broke down from overwork, another third broke down from dissipation, and the other third ruled Germany." I leave it to each of you to decide in which category you will fall.

I do not suggest that our political and public life should be turned over to college-trained experts, nor would I give this university a seat in the Congress, as William and Mary was once represented in the Virginia House of Burgesses, nor would I adopt from the Belgian constitution a provision giving three votes instead of one to college graduates—at least not until more Democrats go to college. But I do hope that you join us.

Our task in this country is to do our best, to serve our nation's interest as we see it, and not to be swayed from our course by the faint-hearted or the unknowing, or the threats of those who would make themselves our foes.

This is not a simple task in a democracy. We cannot open all our books in advance to an adversary who operates in the night, the decisions we make, the weapons we possess, the bargains we will accept—nor can we always see reflected overnight the success or failure of the actions that we may take.

In times past, a simple slogan described our policy: "Fifty-four-forty or fight." "To make the world safe for democracy." "No entangling alliances." But the times, issues, and the weapons, all have changed—and complicate and endanger our lives. It is a dangerous illusion to believe that the policies of the United States, stretching as they do world-wide, under varying and different conditions, can be encompassed in one slogan or one adjective, hard or soft or otherwise—or to believe that we shall soon meet total victory or total defeat.

Peace and freedom do not come cheap, and we are destined, all of us here today, to live most of our lives, if not all of our lives, in uncertainty and challenge and peril. Our policy must therefore blend whatever degree of firmness and flexibility which is necessary to protect our vital interests, by peaceful means if possible, by resolute action if necessary.

We move for the first time in our history through an age in which two opposing powers have the capacity to destroy each other, and while we do not intend to see the free world give up, we shall make every effort to prevent the world from being blown up.

The American eagle on our official seal emphasizes both peace and freedom, and as I said in the State of the Union address, we in this country give equal attention to its claws when it in its left hand holds the arrows and in its right the olive branch.

This is a time of national maturity, understanding, and willingness to face issues as they are, not as we would like them to be. It is a test of our ability to be far-seeing and calm, as well as resolute, to keep an eye on both our dangers and our opportunities, and not to be diverted by momentary gains, or setbacks, or pressures. And it is the long view of the educated citizen to which the graduates of this university can best contribute.

We must distinguish the real from the illusory, the long-range from the temporary, the significant from the petty, but if we can be purposeful, if we can face up to our risks and live up to our word, if we can do our duty undeterred by fanatics or frenzy at home or abroad, then surely peace and freedom will prevail. We shall be neither Red nor dead, but alive and free—and worthy of the traditions and responsibilities of the United States of America.

Remarks in Nashville at the 90th Anniversary Convocation of Vanderbilt University, May 18, 1963

We live in an age of movement and change, both evolutionary and revolutionary, both good and evil—and in such an age a university has a special obligation to hold fast to the best of the past and move fast to the best of the future. . . .

Liberty and learning will be and must be the touchstones of any free university in this country or the world. I say two touchstones, yet they are almost inseparable, inseparable if not indistinguishable, for liberty without learning is always in peril, and learning without liberty is always in vain. . . .

This nation is now engaged in a continuing debate about the rights of a portion of its citizens. That will go on, and those rights will expand until the standard first forged by the nation's founders has been reached, and all Americans enjoy equal opportunity and liberty under law.

But this nation was not founded solely on the principle of citizens' rights. Equally important, though too often not discussed, is the citizen's responsibility. For our privileges can be no greater than our obligations. The protection of our rights can endure no longer than the performance of our responsibilities. Each can be neglected only at the peril of the other. I speak to you today, therefore, not of your rights as Americans, but of your responsibilities. They are many in number and different in nature. They do not rest with equal weight upon the shoulders of all. Equality of opportunity does not mean equality of responsibility. All Americans must be responsible citizens, but some must be more responsible than others, by virtue of their public or their private position, their role in the family or community, their prospects for the future, or their legacy from the past.

25

Increased responsibility goes with increased ability, for "of those to whom much is given, much is required." . . . I speak in particular . . . of the responsibility of the educated citizen. "Every man sent out from a university," said Professor Woodrow Wilson, "Every man sent out from a university should be a man of his nation, as well as a man of his time."

You have responsibilities, in short, to use your talents for the benefit of the society which helped develop those talents. You must decide, as Goethe put it, whether you will be an anvil or a hammer, whether you will give to the world in which you were reared and educated the broadest possible benefits of that education. Of the many special obligations incumbent upon an educated citizen, I would cite three as outstanding: your obligation to the pursuit of learning, your obligation to serve the public, your obligation to uphold the law.

If the pursuit of learning is not defended by the educated citizen, it will not be defended at all. For there will always be those who scoff at intellectuals, who cry out against research, who seek to limit our educational system. Modern cynics and sceptics see no more reason for landing a man on the moon, which we shall do, than the cynics and sceptics of half a millennium ago saw for the discovery of this country. They see no harm in paying those to whom they entrust the minds of their children a smaller wage than is paid to those to whom they entrust their plumbing.

But the educated citizen knows how much more there is to know. He knows that "knowledge is power," more so today than ever before. He knows that only an educated and informed people will be a free people, that the ignorance of one voter in a democracy impairs the security of all, and that if we can, as Jefferson put it, "enlighten the people generally . . . tyranny and the oppressions of mind and body will vanish, like evil spirits at the dawn of day." And, therefore, the educated citizen has a special obligation to encourage the pursuit of learning, to promote exploration of the unknown, to preserve the freedom of inquiry, to support the advancement of research, and to assist at every level of government the improvement of education for all Americans, from grade school to graduate school.

Secondly, the educated citizen has an obligation to serve the public. He may be a precinct worker or President. He may give his talents at the courthouse, the State House, the White House. He may be a civil servant or a senator, a candidate or a campaign worker, a winner or a loser. But he must be a participant and not a spectator.

"At the Olympic games," Aristotle wrote, "it is not the finest and strongest men who are crowned, but they who enter the lists—for out of these the prize men are elected. So, too, in life, of the honorable and the good, it is they who act who rightly win the prizes."

I urge all of you today, especially those who are students, to act, to enter the lists of public service and rightly win or lose the prize. For we can have only one form of aristocracy in this country, as Jefferson wrote long ago in rejecting John Adams' suggestion of an artificial aristocracy of wealth and birth. It is, he wrote, the natural aristocracy of character and talent, and the best form of government, he added, was that which selected these men for positions of responsibility.

I would hope that all educated citizens would fulfill this obligation—in politics, in the Peace Corps, in the Foreign Service, in the Government Service, in the world. You will find the pressures greater than the pay. You may endure more public attacks than support. But you will have the unequaled satisfaction of knowing that your character and talent are contributing to the direction and success of this free society.

Third, and finally, the educated citizen has an obligation to uphold the law. This is the obligation of every citizen in

27

a free and peaceful society, but the educated citizen has a special responsibility by virtue of his greater understanding. For whether he has ever studied history or current events, ethics or civics, the rules of a profession or the tools of a trade, he knows that only a respect for the law makes it possible for free men to dwell together in peace and progress.

He knows that law is the adhesive force in the cement of society, creating order out of chaos and coherence in place of anarchy. He knows that for one man to defy a law or court order he does not like is to invite others to defy those which they do not like, leading to a breakdown of all justice and all order. He knows, too, that every fellow man is entitled to be regarded with decency and treated with dignity. Any educated citizen who seeks to subvert the law, to suppress freedom, or to subject other human beings to acts that are less than human, degrades his heritage, ignores his learning, and betrays his obligation.

Certain other societies may respect the rule of force; we respect the rule of law.

The nation, indeed the whole world, has watched recent events in the United States with alarm and dismay. No one can deny the complexity of the problems involved in assuring to all of our citizens their full rights as Americans. But no one can gainsay the fact that the determination to secure these rights is in the highest traditions of American freedom.

In these moments of tragic disorder, a special burden rests on the educated men and women of our country to reject the temptations of prejudice and violence, and to reaffirm the values of freedom and law on which our free society depends.

Address at the University of California at Berkeley, March 23, 1962

We may be proud as a nation of our record in scientific

28

achievement—but at the same time we must be impressed by the interdependence of all knowledge. I am certain that every scholar and scientist here today would agree that his own work has benefited immeasurably from the work of the men and women in other countries. The prospect of a partnership with Soviet scientists in the exploration of space opens up exciting prospects of collaboration in other areas of learning. And cooperation in the pursuit of knowledge can hopefully lead to cooperation in the pursuit of peace.

Yet the pursuit of knowledge itself implies a world where men are free to follow out the logic of their own ideas. It implies a world where nations are free to solve their own problems and to realize their own ideals. It implies, in short, a world where collaboration emerges from the voluntary decisions of nations strong in their own independence and their own self-respect. It implies, I believe, the kind of world which is emerging before our eyes—the world produced by the revolution of national independence which has today, and has been since 1945, sweeping across the face of the world.

I sometimes think that we are too much impressed by the clamor of daily events. The newspaper headlines and the television screens give us a short view. They so flood us with the stop-press details of daily stories that we lose sight of one of the great movements of history. Yet it is the profound tendencies of history and not the passing excitements that will shape our future.

The short view gives us the impression as a nation of being shoved and harried, everywhere on the defense. But this impression is surely an optical illusion. From the perspective of Moscow, the world today may seem ever more troublesome, more intractable, more frustrating than it does to us. The leaders of the Communist world are confronted not only by acute internal problems in each Communist country —the failure of agriculture, the rising discontent of the youth and the intellectuals, the demands of technical and managerial groups for status and security. They are confronted in addition by profound divisions within the Communist world itself—divisions which have already shattered the image of Communism as a universal system guaranteed to abolish all social and international conflicts—the most valuable asset the Communists had for many years.

Wisdom requires the long view. And the long view shows us that the revolution of national independence is a fundamental fact of our era. This revolution will not be stopped. As new nations emerge from the oblivion of centuries, their first aspiration is to affirm their national identity. Their deepest hope is for a world where, within a framework of international cooperation, every country can solve its own problems according to its own traditions and ideals.

It is in the interests of the pursuit of knowledge—and it is in our own national interest—that this revolution of national independence succeed. For the Communists rest everything on the idea of a monolithic world—a world where all knowledge has a single pattern, all societies move toward a single model, and all problems and roads have a single solution and a single destination. The pursuit of knowledge, on the other hand, rests everything on the opposite idea—on the idea of a world based on diversity, self-determination, freedom. And that is the kind of world to which we Americans, as a nation, are committed by the principles upon which the great Republic was founded.

As men conduct the pursuit of knowledge, they create a world which freely unites national diversity and international partnership. This emerging world is incompatible with the Communist world order. It will irresistibly burst the bonds of the Communist organization and the Communist ideology. And diversity and independence, far from being opposed to the American conception of world order, represent the very essence of our view of the future of the world.

30

There used to be so much talk a few years ago about the inevitable triumph of Communism. We hear such talk much less now. No one who examines the modern world can doubt that the great currents of history are carrying the world away from the monolithic idea toward the pluralistic idea—away from Communism and toward national independence and freedom. No one can doubt that the wave of the future is not the conquest of the world by a single dogmatic creed but the liberation of the diverse energies of free nations and free men. No one can doubt that cooperation in the pursuit of knowledge must lead to freedom of the mind and freedom of the soul.

Beyond the drumfire of daily crisis, therefore, there is arising the outlines of a robust and vital world community, founded on nations secure in their own independence, and united by allegiance to world peace. It would be foolish to say that this world will be won tomorrow, or the day after. The processes of history are fitful and uncertain and aggravating. There will be frustrations and setbacks. There will be times of anxiety and gloom. The spector of thermonuclear war will continue to hang over mankind; and we must heed the advice of Oliver Wendell Holmes of "freedom leaning on her spear" until all nations are wise enough to disarm safely and effectively.

Yet we can have a new confidence today in the direction in which history is moving. Nothing is more stirring than the recognition of great public purpose. Every great age is marked by innovation and daring—by the ability to meet unprecedented problems with intelligent solutions. In a time of turbulence and change, it is more true than ever that knowledge is power; for only by true understanding and steadfast judgment are we able to master the challenge of history.

If this is so, we must strive to acquire knowledge—and to apply it with wisdom. We must reject oversimplified theories

31

of international life—the theory that American power is unlimited, or that the American mission is to remake the world in the American image. We must seize the vision of a free and diverse world—and shape our policies to speed progress toward a more flexible world order.

This is the unifying spirit of our policies in the world today. The purpose of our aid programs must be to help developing countries move forward as rapidly as possible on the road to genuine national independence. Our military policies must assist nations to protect the processes of democratic reform and development against disruption and intervention. Our diplomatic policies must strengthen our relations with the whole world, with our several alliances, and within the United Nations.

As we press forward on every front to realize a flexible world order, the role of the university becomes ever more important, both as a reservoir of ideas and as a repository of the long view of the shore dimly seen.

"Knowledge is the great sun of the firmament," said Senator Daniel Webster. "Life and power are scattered with all its beams."

In its light, we must think and act not only for the moment but for our time. I am reminded of the story of the great French Marshal Lyautey, who once asked his gardener to plant a tree. The gardener objected that the tree was slow-growing and would not reach maturity for a hundred years. The marshal replied, "In that case, there is no time to lose, plant it this afternoon."

Today a world of knowledge—a world of cooperation—a just and lasting peace—may be years away. But we have no time to lose. Let us plant our trees this afternoon.

32

PHYSICAL FITNESS

●

Vigor (or "vigah," as it sounded in the President's Boston accent) became one of the keynotes of the Kennedy administration. At forty-three, Kennedy was the youngest man ever to be elected President, and his vitality pervaded the govern-

33

ment. His physical drive enabled him to maintain a daily schedule that exhausted his associates and the newsmen who followed at his heels.

Kennedy suffered a number of serious illnesses during his childhood and later years, and was twice near death. Each time he pulled through, with determination, and continued leading an active life, full of sports, calisthenics, and exercise. Even with a painful back injury, he swam and did calisthenics daily in the White House. He believed implicitly in the Greek idea of developing the whole man—that physical and mental vigor go together, and are equally important.

Partly because tests showed that Americans fell far below physical fitness standards set by Europeans, Kennedy advocated comprehensive fitness programs in the schools, including fifteen minutes of vigorous activity every day, tests to determine physical abilities and progress, and extra help for people who needed it. Schools all over the country instituted fitness programs, and people from all walks of life adopted the idea and began working on their own physical development programs.

Sports had always been important to the President. Sailing, swimming, tennis, and touch football were sports the whole Kennedy family played hard. When they were children, Jack Kennedy was particularly competitive with his older brother Joe, a fine athlete. At thirteen, Kennedy tried for the football and swimming teams at Canterbury School in Connecticut, and, although he was too small to make the football team, he was clocked at thirty seconds for the fifty-yard dash in swimming. At Choate, which he attended until he graduated, he played football, basketball, golf, and tennis. Later, at Harvard College he won letters in swimming, football, and golf. He also suffered the back injury, playing football, that was to plague him all his life. Although Kennedy was never a star, he was always fiercely competitive. But while winning was important to him, so was playing as well as possible. He well knew the value of the fun and physical benefits of sports in maintaining a healthy society in a tense world, and was disstressed to see a trend toward spectator sports at the expense of amateur athletics. He made the point at the National Football Foundation and Hall of Fame banquet on December 5, 1961. He had just received the group's gold medal, presented each year to a person dedicated to spreading the idea of amateur football.

Politics is an astonishing profession— . . . it's enabled me to go from being an obscure member of the junior varsity at Harvard to being an honorary member of the Football Hall of Fame.

Actually, there are not so many differences between politics and football. Some Republicans have been unkind enough to suggest that my election, which was somewhat close, was somewhat similar to the Notre Dame-Syracuse game. But I'm like Notre Dame, we just take it as it comes and we're not giving it back.

I'm proud to be here tonight. I think General MacArthur, when he was superintendent, really spoke about football in the classic way, because on so many occasions, in war and peace, I have seen so many men who participated in this sport—some celebrated and some obscure—who did demonstrate that the seeds had been well sown.

I am delighted to be here tonight and participating with you. This is a great American game. It has given me, personally, some of the most pleasant moments of my life— from last Saturday when I had a chance to see the Army-Navy game to a Harvard-Yale game I saw forty years before.

And I'm also glad to be here tonight with some men who also gave me some of the most exciting moments of my life. Clint Frank, who I understand is sitting down there, whom I saw score five touchdowns against Princeton. Tom Harmon, who scored twenty-one points on my twenty-first birthday in the first half of a game against California. Cliff Battles, who made George Marshall look good at Boston way back in the thirties. And Jay Berwanger, who's here tonight, who, when Chicago was tenth in the Big Ten, was on everyone's All-American. And Sam Huff, who campaigned with me through the coal mines of West Virginia—and he's even better at that than he is on Sunday.

So I'm like a good many other Americans who never quite made it—but love it.

I do see a close relationship between sports and our national life and I sometimes wonder whether those of us who love sports have done as much as we should in maintaining sports as a constructive part of this country's existence.

I will not enter into a debate about whether football or baseball is our national sport. The sad fact is that it looks more and more as if our national sport is not playing at all —but watching. We have become more and more not a nation of athletes but a nation of spectators.

Professional athletes—professional athletics—I believe has a great place in our national life, but I must confess that I view the growing emphasis on professionalism and specialization in amateur sports without great enthusiasm. Gibbon wrote two centuries ago that professionalism in amateur sports was one of the early evidences of the decline and fall of the Roman Empire.

Football today is far too much a sport for the few who can play it well. The rest of us—and too many of our children—get our exercise from climbing up to seats in stadiums, or from walking across the room to turn on our television sets. And this is true for one sport after another, all across the board.

The result of this shift from participation to, if I may use the word "spectation," is all too visible in the physical condition of our population.

Despite our much-publicized emphasis on school athletics, our own children lag behind European children in physical fitness. And astonishingly enough, when Dr. Kraus and Dr. Weber recently went back, after ten years, to Europe they found a sharp decline in the physical fitness of European children, because in the last decade mechanization had begun to get at them too.

It's no wonder that we have such a high proportion of rejections for physical reasons in our Selective Service. A short time ago General Hershey told me that since October of 1948, of some six million young men examined for military duty, more than a million were rejected as physically unfit for military service. A good many of these men would not have been rejected if they had had an opportunity, when younger, to take part in an adequate physical development program.

To get two men today, the United States Army must call seven men. Of the five rejected, three are turned down for physical reasons and two for mental disabilities. To get the 196,000 additional men that we needed for Berlin, the government had to call up, therefore, 750,000 men—and the rejection rate is increasing each year.

I find this situation disturbing. We are underexercised as a nation. We look instead of play. We ride instead of walk. Our existence deprives us of the minimum of physical activity essential for healthy living. And the remedy, in my judgment, lies in one direction; that is, in developing programs for broad participation in exercise by all of our young men and women—all of our boys and girls.

I do not say this in order to decry excellence in sports or anywhere else. But excellence emerges from mass participa-

37

tion. This is shown by the fact that in some areas of our Olympic Games, we have steadily fallen behind those nations who have stressed broad participation in a great variety of sports.

I believe that as a nation we should give our full support, for example, to our Olympic development program. We will not subsidize our athletes as some nations do, but we should as a country set a goal, not in the way the Soviet Union or the Chinese do, but in the kind of way that Australia and other countries do—perhaps in our own way, to emphasize this most important part of life, the opportunity to exercise, to participate in physical activity, and generally to produce a standard of excellence for our country which will enable our athletes to win the Olympics—but more importantly than that, which will give us a nation of vigorous men and women.

There are more important goals than winning contests, and that is to improve on a broad level the health and vitality of all of our people.

We have begun this year to make progress toward this goal with the new President's Council on Youth Fitness. The idea behind our youth fitness program is to give as many American boys and girls as possible a chance for a healthy physical development.

Coach Bud Wilkinson, who after losing his first five games finally got out of our atmosphere and went on to win his next five, and the Council staff, in cooperation with the nation's leading educators and medical organizations, have worked out a basic physical fitness program for our elementary and secondary schools. Pilot projects have been set up in a number of cities.

The results so far show the effectiveness of what can be done and the extent of the need. In Muskogee, Oklahoma, for example, a city which prides itself on athletic achievement, which has had seven All-Americans in recent years, 47 percent of the students failed a minimum physical fitness test. Only a fraction of those who qualified could pass the more comprehensive test of physical capability. Yet only six weeks of participation in a daily fifteen-minute program of vigorous exercise brought about a 24 percent improvement among those who failed the first test.

Throughout the country we have found equally discouraging examples of deficiency—and equally encouraging examples of progress. I hope that every school district in this country will adopt our minimum program. I urge every parent to support the program and his own children's participation in it. I urge our colleges and universities to lay down basic standards of physical fitness. I urge the nation's community recreation centers to provide more opportunity for those who are no longer attending school. And finally, I urge organizations such as this, with all of the prestige and influence which you bring to American life, to help establish more programs for participation by American boys and girls—by Americans young and old. In short, what we must do is literally change the physical habits of millions of Americans—and that is far more difficult than changing their tastes, their fashions, or even their politics.

I do not suggest that physical development is the central object of life, or that we should permit cultural and intellectual values to be diminished, but I do suggest that physical health and vitality constitute an essential element of a vigorous American community.

No one knew this better than the men of Greece, to whom our civilization owes so much. The Greeks sought excellence not only in philosophy and drama and sculpture and architecture, but in athletics. The same people who produced the poetry of Homer, the wisdom of Plato and Aristotle—they also produced the Olympic Games. The

39

Greeks understood that mind and body must develop in harmonious proportion to produce a creative intelligence. And so did the most brilliant intelligence of our earliest days, Thomas Jefferson, when he said, "Not less than two hours a day should be devoted to exercise." If a man who wrote the Declaration of Independence, was Secretary of State, and twice President could give it two hours, our children can give it ten or fifteen minutes.

There's no reason in the world—and we've seen it tonight—why Americans should not be fine students and fine athletes. When I was young, Barry Wood used to play with Ben Ticknor football for Harvard—and hockey and baseball and tennis. He was a ten-letter man—and also the First Marshal of Phi Beta Kappa. And since then he has combined a life of leadership in the medical profession.

I have in Washington, as you know—and he is a friend of many of you—the Deputy Attorney General, Byron White, who was simultaneously a Rhodes scholar and a halfback for the Detroit Lions, and the year that he led the league in ground gained rushing, was also number one man in his class at the Yale Law School. We can combine and must combine intellectual energy and physical vitality.

Theodore Roosevelt once said, "The credit belongs to the man who is actually in the arena—whose face is marred by dust and sweat and blood . . . who knows the great enthusiasms, the great devotions—and spends himself in a worthy cause—who at best if he wins knows the thrills of high achievement—and if he fails at least fails while daring greatly—so that his place shall never be with those cold and timid souls who know neither victory nor defeat."

The athletes in this room—you gentlemen—and your colleagues across the country have known victory and defeat, and have accepted both. I salute you.

RELIGION

●

Religion was important to President Kennedy, both spiritually and politically. As the second Roman Catholic ever to be nominated for the Presidency, he represented a religious issue that had never been settled: Could a Catholic be President? Many people claimed that a Catholic President might find that his duties to his country conflicted with his allegiance to the Pope as head of the Catholic Church, and that if he was a good Catholic he could therefore not be a good President.

This theory had been a major reason for the fact that no Catholic had successfully run for America's highest office. Kennedy's position was clear from the beginning: "Whatever one's religion in his private life may be, for the officeholder nothing takes precedence over his oath to uphold the Constitution and all its parts," he wrote in Look magazine in March 1959. The issue continued to be raised, however. After a group of prominent Protestant clergymen had made a particularly outspoken attack on the issue, Kennedy made an important speech that summed up his position once and for all:

[It is] not what kind of church I believe in, for that should be important only to me, but what kind of America I believe in.

I believe in an America where the separation of church and state is absolute—where no Catholic prelate would tell the President (should he be Catholic) how to act, and no Protestant minister would tell his parishioners for whom to vote—where no church or church school is granted any public funds or political preference . . . an America that is officially neither Catholic, Protestant, nor Jewish—where no public official either requests or accepts instructions on public policy from . . . any . . . ecclesiastical source . . . where there is no Catholic vote, no anti-Catholic vote, no bloc voting of any kind . . . and where religious liberty is so indivisible that an act against one church is treated as an act against all. . . . I am not the Catholic candidate for President, I am the Democratic Party's candidate for President

42

who happens also to be a Catholic. I do not speak for my church on public matters, and the church does not speak for me. (Ministerial Association, Houston, Texas, September 12, 1960.)

Aside from its political implications, Kennedy's faith was very important to him. Although he kept his religion private, the President did make clear from time to time how important it was to him, in speeches like this one, delivered at a dedication breakfast of the International Christian Leadership on February 9, 1961:

This country was founded by men and women who were dedicated or came to be dedicated to two propositions: first, a strong religious conviction, and secondly, a recognition that this conviction could flourish only under a system of freedom.

I think it is appropriate that we pay tribute to this great constitutional principle which is enshrined in the First Amendment of the Constitution: the principle of religious independence, of religious liberty, of religious freedom. But I think it is also important that we pay tribute and acknowledge another great principle, and that is the principle of religious conviction. Religious freedom has no significance unless it is accompanied by conviction. And therefore the Puritans and the Pilgrims of my own section of New England, the Quakers of Pennsylvania, the Catholics of Maryland, the Presbyterians of North Carolina, the Methodists and the Baptists who came later, all shared these two great traditions which, like silver threads, have run through the warp and the woof of American history.

No man who enters upon the office to which I have succeeded can fail to recognize how every President of the United States has placed special reliance upon his faith in God. Every President has taken comfort and courage when told, as we are told today, that the Lord "will be with thee. He will not fail thee nor forsake thee. Fear not—neither be thou dismayed."

While they came from a wide variety of religious backgrounds and held a wide variety of religious beliefs, each of our Presidents in his own way has placed a special trust in God. Those who were strongest intellectually were also strongest spiritually.

Today our nation is passing through another time of trial. In many ways, our dangers and our problems are far greater —and certainly infinitely more complex. We will need to draw upon the best that this nation has—often—and draw upon it physically and intellectually and materially.

But we need also to call upon our great reservoir of spiritual resources. We must recognize that human collaboration is not enough, that in times such as these we must reach beyond ourselves if we are to seek ultimate courage and infinite wisdom.

It is an ironic fact that in this nuclear age, when the horizon of human knowledge and human experience has passed far beyond any that any age has ever known, that we turn back at this time to the oldest source of wisdom and strength, to the words of the prophets and the saints, who tell us that faith is more powerful than doubt, that hope is more potent than despair, and that only through the love that is sometimes called charity can we conquer those forces within ourselves and throughout all the world that threaten the very existence of mankind.

Keeping in mind that "when a man's ways please the Lord, he maketh even his enemies to be at peace with him," let us go forth to lead this land that we love, joining in the prayer of General George Washington in 1783, "that God would have you in His holy protection, that He would incline the hearts of the citizens . . . to entertain a brotherly

44

love and affection one for another . . . and finally that He would most graciously be pleased to dispose us all to do justice, to love mercy, and to demean ourselves with . . . the characteristics of the Divine Author of our blessed religion, without an humble imitation of whose example we can never hope to be a happy nation."

The guiding principle and prayer of this nation has been, is now, and shall ever be "In God We Trust."

THE ARTS

●

John and Jacqueline Kennedy's interest in the arts created in the White House a national center of culture such as it had never been before. To both the Kennedys, brought up in an atmosphere of culture, the arts were an essential part of life, and to the President they represented a central facet of the national spirit. On his inauguration day, Kennedy gave recognition to the important role art plays in society by asking the poet Robert Frost to read a poem and inviting more than fifty of the nation's outstanding writers, painters, and composers to attend the inaugural ceremonies.

One of many ways in which Kennedy promoted the arts was to invite prominent musicians, actors, and authors to perform at the White House. There, before the President and important guests, cellist Pablo Casals played his first concert in the United States after more than thirty years of voluntary exile. Igor Stravinsky, André Malraux, and Thornton Wilder were among the other artists honored at the White House. In such glittering social and intellectual surroundings the performing arts took on a prestige and a prominence that they had not enjoyed since the earliest days of the republic. Recognition was given to the Nobel Prize winners of the Western Hemisphere at a famous dinner that the President called "the most extraordinary collection of talent, of human knowledge, that has ever been gathered together at the White House, with the possible exception of when Thomas Jefferson dined alone."

At a commemorative service for Robert Frost at Amherst College in Massachusetts on October 26, 1963, President Kennedy expressed his concept of the importance of the artist in society:

In America, our heroes have customarily run to men of large accomplishments. But today this college and country honors a man whose contribution was not to our size but to our spirit, not to our political beliefs but to our insight, not to our self-esteem, but to our self-comprehension. In honoring Robert Frost, we therefore can pay honor to the deepest sources of our national strength. That strength takes many forms, and the most obvious forms are not always the most

47

significant. The men who create power make an indispensable contribution to the nation's greatness, but the men who question power make a contribution just as indispensable, especially when that questioning is disinterested, for they determine whether we use power or power uses us.

Our national strength matters, but the spirit which informs and controls our strength matters just as much. This was the special significance of Robert Frost. He brought an unsparing instinct for reality to bear on the platitudes and pieties of society. His sense of the human tragedy fortified him against self-deception and easy consolation. "I have been," he wrote, "one acquainted with the night." And because he knew the midnight as well as the high noon, because he understood the ordeal as well as the triumph of the human spirit, he gave his age strength with which to overcome despair. At bottom, he held a deep faith in the spirit of man, and it is hardly an accident that Robert Frost coupled poetry and power, for he saw poetry as the means of saving power from itself. When power leads man toward arrogance, poetry reminds him of his limitations. When power narrows the areas of man's concern, poetry reminds him of the richness and diversity of his existence. When power corrupts, poetry cleanses. For art establishes the basic human truth which must serve as the touchstone of our judgment.

The artist, however faithful to his personal vision of reality, becomes the last champion of the individual mind and sensibility against an intrusive society and an officious state. The great artist is thus a solitary figure. He has, as Frost said, a lover's quarrel with the world. In pursuing his perceptions of reality, he must often sail against the currents of his time. This is not a popular role. If Robert Frost was much honored during his lifetime, it was because a good many preferred to ignore his darker truths. Yet in retrospect, we see how the artist's fidelity has strengthened the fiber of our national life.

If sometimes our great artists have been the most critical of our society, it is because their sensitivity and their concern for justice, which must motivate any true artist, makes him aware that our nation falls short of its highest potential. I see little of more importance to the future of our country and our civilization than full recognition of the place of the artist.

If art is to nourish the roots of our culture, society must set the artist free to follow his vision wherever it takes him. We must never forget that art is not a form of propaganda; it is a form of truth. And as Mr. MacLeish once remarked of poets, "There is nothing worse for our trade than to be in style." In free society art is not a weapon and it does not belong to the sphere of polemics and ideology. Artists are not engineers of the soul. It may be different elsewhere. But democratic society—in it, the highest duty of the writer, the composer, the artist is to remain true to himself and to let the chips fall where they may. In serving his vision of the truth, the artist best serves his nation. And the nation which disdains the mission of art invites the fate of Robert Frost's hired man, the fate of having "nothing to look backward to with pride, and nothing to look forward to with hope."

I look forward to a great future for America, a future in which our country will match its military strength with our moral restraint, its wealth with our wisdom, its power with our purpose. I look forward to an America which will not be afraid of grace and beauty, which will protect the beauty of our national environment, which will preserve the great old American houses and squares and parks of our national past, and which will build handsome and balanced cities for our future.

I look forward to an America which will reward achievement in the arts as we reward achievement in business or statecraft. I look forward to an America which will steadily raise the standards of artistic accomplishment and which will steadily enlarge cultural opportunities for all of our citizens. And I look forward to an America which commands respect throughout the world not only for its strength but for its civilization as well. And I look forward to a world which will be safe not only for democracy and diversity but also for personal distinction.

At some of the many White House concerts given by students the President expressed his feelings about involvement in music.

One of our great assets in this country are the talented boys and girls who devote their early lives to music, to appreciation of music, to an understanding of it. This is a great and I think vital force in American life. It is a part of American life which I think is unheralded around the world. But this emphasis upon artistic achievement in music I think is a source of satisfaction and pride to all of us. *(White House Musical Program for Youth, April 16, 1962)*

I know that there is some feeling by Americans that the arts are developed in solitude, that they are developed by inspiration and by sudden fits of genius. But the fact of the matter is that success comes in music or in the arts like success comes in every other form of human endeavor—by hard work, by discipline, over a long period of time. Every musician here, every musician in the United States, every musician in the world plays after months and years of the most painstaking work, the kind of discipline which most people cannot endure. So I hope when you see them that you will realize that they are not playing merely because they happen to have natural talent, but they are playing be-

50

cause their natural talent was developed by their own sense of discipline.

In addition, we're glad to have them here because I think they symbolize a great artistic movement which is so strong in the United States. There are over 33 million Americans who are interested in music, interested in other art forms. That is a tremendous statistic. That does not say that 33 million Americans play well. I was once, when I was younger, one of those statistics which were thrown around so casually in those days. That does not mean that 33 million can play so that you want to hear them, but they play because they want to hear themselves, and perhaps that's the best form of art expression. *(White House Concert by the National High School Symphony Orchestra, August 6, 1962)*

Besides inviting performers to the White House, the President took other steps to foster the arts in national life. One was the promotion of the National Cultural Center, a project begun by President Eisenhower. In a closed-circuit television broadcast on behalf of the center, on November 9, 1962, Kennedy outlined the importance of culture in the history and life of a nation.

I want to assure the officials of my administration tonight that this demonstration of support for the arts is modest and painless compared to what has been required of past governments and past administrations.

In 1664, Louis XIV, in his own efforts to encourage the arts, donned brilliant tights and played in a drama called "Furious Roland" before a happy court. Moreover, he drafted the highest offices of his administration for the play so that, according to an account, all clad in brilliant tights themselves they passed before the queen and the court.

51

This was suggested tonight but for some reason or other the committee turned it down. But we are glad to be here in any case. And we are glad to be the guests of honor of the representatives of much of the finest in American culture and much of the finest in American life. And we are very much indebted to all the artists who have so willingly taken part in this work tonight. For when Thomas Jefferson wrote that the one thing which from the heart he envied certain other nations, and that was their art, he spoke from a deep understanding of the enduring sources of national greatness and national achievement.

But our culture and art do not speak to America alone. To the extent that artists struggle to express beauty in form and color and sound, to the extent that they write about man's struggle with nature or society, or himself, to that extent they strike a responsive chord in all humanity. Today, Sophocles speaks to us from more than 2,000 years. And in our own time, even when political communications have been strained, the Russian people have bought more than 20,000 copies of the works of Jack London, more than 10 million books of Mark Twain, and hundreds and thousands of copies of Hemingway, Steinbeck, Whitman, and Poe; and our own people, through the works of Tolstoy and Dostoievsky and Pasternak have gained an insight into the shared problems of the human heart.

Thus today, as always, art knows no national boundaries.

Genius can speak at any time, and the entire world will hear it and listen. Behind the storm of daily conflict and crisis, the dramatic confrontations, the tumult of political struggle, the poet, the artist, the musician, continues the quiet work of centuries, building bridges of experience between peoples, reminding man of the universality of his feelings and desires and despairs, and reminding him that the forces that unite are deeper than those that divide.

Thus, art and the encouragement of art is political in the most profound sense, not as a weapon in the struggle, but as an instrument of understanding of the futility of struggle between those who share man's faith. Aeschylus and Plato are remembered today long after the triumphs of imperial Athens are gone. Dante outlived the ambitions of thirteenth-century Florence. Goethe stands serenely above the politics of Germany, and I am certain that after the dust of centuries has passed over our cities, we, too, will be remembered not for victories or defeats in battle or in politics, but for our contribution to the human spirit.

It was Pericles' proudest boast that politically Athens was the school of Hellas. If we can make our country one of the great schools of civilization, then on that achievement will surely rest our claim to the ultimate gratitude of mankind. Moreover, as a great democratic society, we have a special responsibility to the arts, for art is the great democrat calling forth creative genius from every sector of society, disregarding race or religion or wealth or color. The mere accumulation of wealth and power is available to the dictator and the democrat alike. What freedom alone can bring is the liberation of the human mind and spirit which finds its greatest flowering in the free society.

Thus, in our fulfillment of these responsibilities toward the arts lies our unique achievement as a free society.

CITIZENSHIP AND PUBLIC SERVICE

●

John Kennedy grew up in a family heavily involved with politics and public service. His grandfather Patrick J. Kennedy was a state senator and "boss" of a political ward in Boston. His grandfather John F. ("Honey Fitz") Fitzgerald was a colorful politician who was a state senator, a U.S. Congressman, and a three-term mayor of Boston. Kennedy's father served as President Franklin D. Roosevelt's first chairman of the Securities and Exchange Commission and as Ambassador to Great Britain. The Kennedy children were encouraged by their parents to take an interest in current affairs, and John Kennedy had a unique opportunity to see history happening when his father sent him to Europe a few months before World War II began. When he returned to Harvard for his senior year, he wrote a thesis showing why England had not been prepared for war. His astute analysis, published as a book called *Why England Slept,* became a bestseller.

Interested though he was in the forces that shape world affairs, John Kennedy did not have a political career in mind until his older brother Joe was killed in the war. Joe had been slated to be the family politician—now Jack took his place.

In 1946 John Kennedy was elected to the United States House of Representatives, helped by his brother Robert as campaign manager. He was re-elected twice, than ran successfully for the Senate in 1952. He lost a bid for the Vice-Presidential nomination in 1956, but was re-elected to the Senate. He was elected President of the United States in 1960.

Although his own chosen role was that of a politician, Kennedy believed that his was only one kind of contribution that people can make to society. A democracy requires an interest and participation in public affairs by all its citizens, since it is they who determine what their country is to be and do. Kennedy spoke often of the need for every citizen to live up to his obligations, whatever his role. He made the point at the National Convention of the Catholic Youth Organization, November 15, 1963:

I can't imagine a greater cause in which to be engaged, to give the best that you have, for the United States. Be-

55

cause upon the United States rests not only the burdens of caring for 190 million people but also for hundreds of millions of people around the globe who today without hope look to the United States. Whatever we are able to do in this country, whatever success we are able to make of ourselves, whatever leadership we are able to give, whatever demonstration we can make that a free society can function and move ahead and provide a better life for its people—all those things we do here have their effect all around the globe.

The world is engaged in the most difficult and trying struggle in its long history. All of the great epics which have torn the world for the last 2,000 years pale in comparison to the great ideological gulf which separates us from those who oppose us. It is our responsibility not merely to denounce our enemies and those who make themselves our enemies but to make this system work, to demonstrate what freedom can do, what those who are committed to freedom and the future can do. . . .

Winston Churchill once said that democracy is the worst form of government except for all the other systems that have been tried. It is the most difficult. It requires more of you—discipline, character, self-restraint, a willingness to serve the public interest as well as your own private interests. We expect something of you. And unless in this free country of ours we are able to demonstrate that we are able to make this society work and progress, unless we can hope that from you we are going to get back all of the talents which society has helped develop in you, then, quite obviously, all the hopes of all of us that freedom will not only endure but prevail, of course, will be disappointed.

So we ask the best of you. I hope you will spend your time well now, but I hope that in a long life you will recognize your obligations to the great Republic and to help those who need help, to help those millions of boys and girls who drop out of school, who can't find work, who live in underprivileged areas.

I have been impressed by the fact that we have been able to get 10,000 young men and women to go around the world as part of the Peace Corps. But look at all the sections of the United States, in our large cities, in eastern Kentucky, parts of southern Illinois, parts of Ohio, West Virginia, where people live lives of desperation without hope; they look to this country, they look to you, and they look to me to serve. So I hope that all of you will serve— serve not only your families, and your church, but also serve this country. It deserves the best. It has been very generous to us all. And we must be generous in return.

February 1, 1963

Kennedy was very concerned that people continue to be interested in serving the country, and particularly in leadership capacities. He told a group of young people who had gone to Washington to study the workings of the government how desperately well-informed people were needed:

This country has passed through very difficult times in the last fifteen years and is passing through difficult times today. There is no assurance, unfortunately, by the time that you reach positions of responsibility in our country that we will have moved into any safe harbors.

Each generation of public officials, each generation of citizens faces new problems. The solution of every problem brings with it a response which presents new difficulties to our country. But as long as we are—though 6 percent of the world's population, only 180 million people—as long as we are the great defenders of freedom around the world, which I prophesy we will continue to be, we will have the need for the services of devoted citizens.

I hope that you will decide to give some of your life to public service, that some of you will run for office, that others of you will work in the Peace Corps, that others of you will work in your own home towns and decide that every American, in addition to pursuing his own private interests, owes an obligation to maintain this free country of ours.

This is a free society. You can do it whether you want to or not, but I hope you decide to serve the United States in its great years.

August 28, 1962

There is some feeling, I know, by a good many Americans, that the American Constitution, which Gladstone called the most notable work ever struck off by the mind of man, gives us an automatic light to the future, guides our way, and that all we have to do is follow the very clear precepts it lays down for us.

Well, the American Constitution is an extraordinary document and it is certainly the most extraordinary written constitution in the history of the world, but it has required men to make it work, and it still does today. After all, the Constitution was written for an entirely different period in our nation's history. It was written under entirely different conditions. It was written during a period of isolation. It was written at a time when there were thirteen different units which had to be joined together and which, of course, were extremely desirous of limiting the central power of the government.

That Constitution has served us extremely well, but all of

its clauses, the general welfare and due process and the rest, had to be interpreted by man and had to be made to work by men. And it has to be made to work today in an entirely different world from the days in which it was written, both at home and abroad.

I am always struck by the fact that the United States, which has had so many gifted political leaders, in the days before the war, beginning in 1860 and '61, that we had for a period of thirty years in the Congress the most extraordinarily gifted figures that we've had in our history—Calhoun, Clay, Douglas, Benton, and all the rest; and yet they dealt in their whole life, and many of them stayed in the Congress for a generation, with only three or four problems: tariffs, states rights, and the new states coming in, slavery, currency, and two or three others, and yet this extraordinarily gifted group of men failed, and as a result, of course, we had this long and bloody war.

Now, perhaps, our political leaders may not be so gifted, and yet they deal with questions which are far more complex than the questions which came across the desks of our people a century ago.

We deal with questions of monetary and fiscal policy. We deal with questions which are esoteric—balance of payments, nuclear tests, the mix of our strategic weapons. We have obligations stretching all around the globe, and yet this country must make not only our society work, but all those societies which are dependent upon us.

This is an extraordinary obligation which presses upon those who hold positions of responsibility in the national government today. And where these rather towering figures of a century ago failed in dealing with the relatively few and, in a way, obvious questions with which they had to deal, now the questions which come across our desks and, therefore, really, in a sense, the desk of every citizen, every active voter, dwarf in complexity and in importance all that went then. . . .

I know that perhaps a generation ago, a government career was regarded in a sense for those who wanted the more secure and steady life. That isn't true, of course, today. Whether you serve the government abroad—and I can assure you it isn't a place for those who prefer the gentle winds—I think whether you work for the United States abroad or whether you work here in Washington or any place, this is the most challenging career that could possibly be before any American. And while the compensation may not be as great—the immediate financial compensation—nevertheless the rewards are unlimited.

So I hope that those of you who can will come back here. Those of you who cannot will choose some other way of serving the general interest. For the next ten to twenty years the burdens will be placed completely upon our country for the preservation of freedom. We stand in the center and we are associated with allies, we are associated with those who are neutral but who are friendly with us, we are associated with those who have a latent hostility to us, but all depends upon the keystone which is the Uinted States. And that is a sober responsibility for a country which twenty years ago prided itself on its long isolationist and neutralist tradition. . . .

Woodrow Wilson once said that every man sent out from a university should be a man of his nation as well as a man of his time. Those of you who have the advantage of college educations and work here I think can represent the best kind of civil servant or politician. It is an attractive career, I assure you, and I wouldn't want anyone to sit on the sidelines today when so much goes on in the mainstream.

August 27, 1963

The government of the United States is a most complex institution. It is an unfortunate fact of history, as we look around the world, that the number of people who are able to maintain this sensitive system of democracy and individual liberty is rather limited. It has been confined, on the whole, to a relatively few areas of the world. Most of the world moves through a far more centralized system of authority which takes the ultimate responsibility upon the government and not upon the people themselves.

To make this sensitive, difficult, and complicated system, which demands so much of us in the qualities of self-restraint and self-discipline, to make it possible for us to live together in harmony, to carry out those policies which provide domestic tranquility here at home, and security for us abroad, requires the best of all of us.

I can assure you that there is no career which you can adopt, when you leave college, that will bring you a more and greater sense of satisfaction and a greater feeling of participation in a great effort than will your work here or in your state or in your community.

We sometimes think that the past days were the golden days, that the great figures in the Senate, or the great Presidents, were the great Presidents and the great Senators. This may be true, but the fact of the matter is that the problems we deal with, however adequately or inadequately, the problems that we deal with in the 1960's dwarf all of the problems which this country dealt with, with the possible exception of the problems a hundred years ago. Other than that, this generation of Americans—you here who will be in positions of responsibility for the rest of this century—will deal with the most difficult, sensitive, and dangerous problems that any society of people has ever dealt with in any age.

The fact of the matter is, through the whole 19th century this country dealt with only five or six major problems —the right of states, the whole question of slavery—which was tied with states' rights—the tariff, the development of the West, currency problems. In a generalized way those were the major issues of the 19th century, and Calhoun and Webster and Clay, who came to the Congress in the period 1810, 1811, or 1812, were talking about the same problems —the same four or five problems forty years later in 1850— when they dominated the Senate.

Now the problems come pouring across the desks of the American people, in even a summer, which deal again with the right of states, with the whole problem of space, and our balance of payments, and what happens in the Middle East, and the relationships between Saudi Arabia and Yemen, or Latin America, or in the Far East, or in Saigon—problems which we can deal with in only a limited way, but problems which affect the security of the United States.

So, therefore, we have these highly complex, highly sophisticated questions upon which experts differ, and yet upon which, if our society is to have a solid foundation, the American people must make a final judgment. Even the discussions and debates upon the test ban only indicate, only suggest the complexities of the problems about which we must make up our minds.

As Mendes France said a decade ago, "To govern is to choose." . . .

How does a Senator, how does a President, how do the people of the United States make a final judgment? There is, of course, no easy answer. What requires is, finally, a choice about what your estimate is of the great movements of history, or the immediate movements, the security of your country, its well-being, the prospects for peace, the dangers of war, and the hope that it is possible to make progress in this rather small globe.

Now, to make a judgment on that, or on balance of payments, or on what actions the Federal Government should take this summer in order to prevent economic downturn in 1964, what is the mix of fiscal and monetary policy which the situation requires in 1963 when, once again, the experts differ? And they can be summoned to every office here or on [Capitol] Hill and they will come to a different conclusion. That requires the best talent that we can get to come to Washington—and to stay home—but in any case to participate, to be not only an acquiescent bystander, but to be a participant who has a feeling, who takes a part, who doesn't read a daily column and have his mind made up for him but, instead, attempts to the best of his ability to understand the great issues and, then, to attempt to have his view carried out, and not to leave it to those who have a specialized interest, who pour mail upon us, inundate us, with their views, while the majority of the American people are unheard of. So that is what we are asking you to come back to this place and work on.

The Greeks defined happiness as the full use of your powers along lines of excellence, and I can imagine no place where you can use your powers more fully along lines of excellence in the 1960's than to be in the service of the United States.

Asked by a Parade magazine correspondent what advice or guidance he would give to a future President, John Kennedy had this to say in 1962:

The first lesson of the Presidency is that it is impossible to foretell the precise nature of the problems that will confront you or the specific skills and capacities which those problems will demand. It is an office which called upon a man of peace, Lincoln, to become a great leader in a bloody war; which required a profound believer in limiting the scope of federal government, Jefferson, to expand dramatically the powers and range of that government; which challenged a man dedicated to domestic social reform, Franklin Roosevelt, to lead this nation into a deep and irrevocable involvement in world affairs. And when you assume the Presidency you too will face problems, difficulties, crises, and challenges which no one can now forsee.

In 1645, John Winthrop, Deputy Governor of Massachusetts Bay Colony, after a long and stormy trial acquitting him of impeachment for exceeding his authority, reminded his fellow citizens that "when you call one to be a magistrate, he doth not profess nor undertake to have sufficient skill for that office, nor can you furnish him with gifts . . . therefore you must run the hazard of his skill and ability."

This insight into the nature of governing affirms the lesson of our history that there is no program of vocational training for the Presidency; no specific area of knowledge that is peculiarly relevant. Nor are qualities of great leadership drawn from any particular section of the country or section of society. Nine of our Presidents, among them some of the most brilliant in office, did not attend college; whereas Thomas Jefferson was one of the great scholars of the age and Woodrow Wilson the president of Princeton University. We have had Presidents who were lawyers and soldiers and teachers. One was an engineeer and another a journalist. They have been drawn from the wealthiest and most distinguished families of the nation, and have come from poor and anonymous beginnings. Some, seemingly well endowed with great abilities and fine qualities, were unable to cope with the demands of the office, while others rose to a greatness far beyond any expectation.

Thus I cannot counsel you about what subjects to study or what vocation to follow. But whatever you do you would be well advised to practice stern discipline and vigorous, unremitting effort. For high qualities and great achievements are not merely matters of chance or birth. They are the product of long and disciplined toil.

Yet, in a more general way, there are experiences which you can pursue, experiences which will support you in the conduct of your great office.

It will help you to know the country you seek to lead. It was one of the great strengths of a President such as Theodore Roosevelt that he knew and loved the diverse magnificence of our fields and mountain ranges, deserts and great rivers, our abundant farmlands and the thousand voices of our cities. No revolution in communication or transportation can destroy the fact that this continent is, as Whitman said, "a nation of nations," which you must see and know before you can govern.

Nor is it accidental that many of our outstanding Presidents, men such as Jefferson or Wilson or Truman, have had a deep sense of history. For of all the disciplines, the study of the folly and achievements of man is best calculated to help develop the critical sense of what is permanent and meaningful amid the mass of superficial and transient events and decisions which engulf the Presidency. And it is on this sense, more than any other, that great leadership depends.

Most important of all, and most difficult to consciously pursue, is an understanding of the people you will lead. You, and at times you alone, will be the spokesman for the great and often silent majority. And the final measure of your administration will, in large measure, rest on how well you respond to their inward hopes while leading them toward new horizons of ambition and achievement. Perhaps you will derive this quality from your origins, as did Lincoln; or from the application of understanding and compassion to the problems of government, as did Franklin Roosevelt. Yet, although the possible sources of this understanding are many, if you find the opportunity to know and work with Americans of diverse backgrounds, occupations and beliefs, then I would urge you to take eagerly that opportunity to enrich yourself.

As a great world leader you will have problems and responsibilities which were not faced by Presidents throughout much of our history. As President of the United States you are a focus of the attention, ambitions, and desires of people and nations throughout the world. It will help you to travel and to learn about these other lands. For the welfare and security of the United States, the future of your own country, is bound to your capacity to exercise leadership and judgment on a global scale.

The most important human qualities of leadership are best embodied in that most towering of American Presidents, Lincoln: a combination of humility and self-confidence, inner resolution and energy, which gives a President the capacity to listen to others, to be aware of his own limitations, but also to follow the command of John Adams that "in all great and essential measures the President is bound by honor and his conscience . . . to act on his own mature and unbiased judgment." I can advise you to be aware of the importance of these qualities, but no one can tell you how to develop them. I only hope, for the welfare of our country, that you will possess them when you come to office.

No one can guarantee that if you follow this or any other advice you will become a great President. For the presidency is peculiarly an office which is shaped by the individual who holds it. And greatness depends on the times as well as the man. But if you work toward your goal, practice dis-

66

cipline and unremitting effort, wish Godspeed to those who will hold and protect the great office of the Republic so that it may pass unimpaired to you and those who will follow you, then, if some chance keeps you from the Presidency, you will still know that you are prepared to serve well your nation as a citizen.

THE PEACE CORPS

●

The Peace Corps is one of President Kennedy's finest legacies. This agency, through which individuals devote their energies and talents directly to serving underdeveloped nations that have requested help, epitomizes his idea of contributing to the welfare of the nation and of the world.

A youth corps had been proposed in the Senate and the House of Representatives in 1960, and during his campaign for the Presidency, Senator Kennedy outlined his vision of American youth working abroad, in a "Message to the Nation's New Voters" on October 5, 1960:

My Democratic colleagues Senator [Hubert] Humphrey and Representative [Henry] Reuss [have proposed] that some appropriate way be found to take advantage of the skills, the talents, the devotion, and the idealism which is inherent in America's young people; and to utilize the services of those properly trained, on the new frontiers of the underdeveloped world—which are in fact the new frontiers of humanity—to aid in building dams, teaching schools, operating hospitals, establishing irrigation projects, and to generally help other people to help themselves.

Should I be elected to provide the Presidential leadership of our nation for the next four years, I would explore thoroughly the possibility of utilizing the services of the very best of our trained and qualified young people to give from three to five years of their lives to the cause of world peace by forming themselves into a Youth Peace Corps, going to the places that really need them and doing the sort of jobs that need to be done.

Young people responded enthusiastically to the idea, and on October 14 he challenged a group of students at the University of Michigan with the concept:

How many of you are willing to spend ten years in Africa or Latin America or Asia working for the U.S. and working for freedom? How many of you [who] are going to be doctors are willing to spend your days in Ghana? Technicians or engineers, how many of you are willing to work in the foreign service, and spend your lives traveling around

69

the world? On your willingness to do that, not merely serve one or two years in the service, but on your willingness to contribute part of your life to this country, I think, will depend the answer whether we as a free society can compete. I think we can, and I think Americans are willing to contribute, but the effort must be far greater than we have made in the past.

The students greeted the idea with a tremendous ovation. Two weeks later, on November 2, 1960, Senator Kennedy formally proposed the Peace Corps as part of his campaign platform in a speech in San Francisco:

We are going to have to have the best Americans we can get to speak for our country abroad. All of us have admired what Dr. Tom Dooley has done in Laos. And others have been discouraged at the examples that we read of the ugly American. And I think that the United States is going to have to do much better in this area if we are going to defend freedom and peace in the 1960's. For the fact of the matter is that out of Moscow and Peiping and Czechoslovakia and East Germany are [coming] hundreds of men and women; scientists, teachers, engineers, doctors, nurses, prepared to spend their lives abroad in the service of world Communism. A friend of mine visiting the Soviet Union last summer met a young Russian couple studying Swahili and African customs at the Moscow Institute of Languages. They were not language teachers. He was a sanitation engineer and she was a nurse, and they were being prepared to live their lives in Africa as missionaries for world Communism.

This can only be countered by the skill and dedication of Americans who are willing to spend their lives serving the cause of freedom.

Wide publicity in the press brought Kennedy's idea of the Peace Corps both nationwide praise and criticism. Letters poured in from people who, finding in the idea the perfect way to work for world peace and understanding, wished to volunteer for service in an organization that so far existed only in the minds of a few statesmen. Meanwhile some columnists and politicians, as well as many private citizens, were calling the idea wildly idealistic and impractical. Press Secretary Pierre Salinger reported that President-elect Kennedy received more mail on the subject of the Peace Corps than on any other issue in his campaign.

The establishment of the Peace Corps was one of the projects foremost in the mind of the new President. While studies were being finished and plans drawn up, he told the country in his State of the Union message of the plan which had already captured the imagination of so many:

An even more valuable asset is our reservoir of dedicated men and women—not only on our college campuses, but in every age group—who have indicated their desire to contribute their skills, their efforts, and a part of their lives to the fight for world order. We can mobilize this talent through the formation of a National Peace Corps, enlisting the services of all those with the desire and capacity to help foreign lands meet their urgent needs for trained personnel.

Backed by the enthusiasm of the President and the eagerness of thousands of volunteers, the plan went forward with remarkable speed. On March 1, 1961, four months after his election, President Kennedy signed Executive Order 10924, establishing the Peace Corps as an agency within the Department of State. A public statement accompanied the order:

I have today signed an Executive Order providing for the establishment of a Peace Corps on a temporary pilot basis.

I am also sending to Congress a message proposing authorization of a permanent Peace Corps. This Corps will be a pool of trained American men and women sent overseas by the U.S. Government or through private institutions and organizations to help foreign countries meet their urgent needs for skilled manpower.

It is our hope to have 500 or more people in the field by the end of the year.

The initial reactions to the Peace Corps proposal are convincing proof that we have, in this country, an immense reservoir of such men and women anxious to sacrifice their energies and time and toil to the cause of world peace and human progress.

In establishing our Peace Corps we intend to make full use of the resources and talents of private institutions and groups. Universities, voluntary agencies, labor unions, and industry will be asked to share in this effort—contributing diverse sources of energy and imagination—making it clear that the responsibility for peace is the responsibility of our entire society.

We will only send abroad Americans who are wanted by the host country—who have a real job to do—and who are qualified to do that job. Programs will be developed with care, and after full negotiation, in order to make sure that the Peace Corps is wanted and will contribute to the welfare of other people. Our Peace Corps is not designed as an instrument of diplomacy or propaganda or ideological conflict. It is designed to permit our people to exercise more fully their responsibilities in the great common cause of world development.

Life in the Peace Corps will not be easy. There will be no salary, and allowances will be at a level sufficient only to maintain health and meet basic needs. Men and women will be expected to work and live alongside the nationals of the country in which they are stationed—doing the same work, eating the same food, talking the same language.

But if the life will not be easy, it will be rich and satisfying. For every young American who participates in the Peace Corps—who works in a foreign land—will know that he or she is sharing in the great common task of bringing to man that decent way of life which is the foundation of freedom and a condition of peace.

Special Message to the Congress on the Peace Corps, March 1, 1961

I recommend to the Congress the establishment of a permanent Peace Corps—a pool of trained American men and women sent overseas by the U.S. Government or through private organizations and institutions to help foreign countries meet their urgent needs for skilled manpower.

I have today signed an Executive Order establishing a Peace Corps on a temporary pilot basis.

The temporary Peace Corps will be a source of information and experience to aid us in formulating more effective plans for a permanent organization. In addition, by starting the Peace Corps now we will be able to begin training young men and women for overseas duty this summer with the objective of placing them in overseas positions by late fall. This temporary Peace Corps is being established under existing authority in the Mutual Security Act and will be located in the Department of State. Its initial expenses will be paid from appropriations currently available for our foreign aid programs.

Throughout the world the people of the newly developing nations are struggling for economic and social progress which reflects their deepest desires. Our own freedom, and the future freedom around the world, depends, in a very real sense, on their ability to build growing and independent nations where men can live in dignity, liberated from the bonds of hunger, ignorance, and poverty.

One of the greatest obstacles to the achievement of this goal is the lack of trained men and women with the skill to teach the young and assist in the operation of development projects—men and women with the capacity to cope with the demands of swiftly evolving economies, and with the dedication to put that capacity to work in the villages, the mountains, the towns, and the factories of dozens of struggling nations.

The vast task of economic development urgently requires skilled people to do the work of the society—to help teach in the schools, construct development projects, demonstrate modern methods of sanitation in the villages, and perform a hundred other tasks calling for training and advanced knowledge.

To meet this urgent need for skilled manpower we are proposing the establishment of a Peace Corps—an organization which will recruit and train American volunteers, sending them abroad to work with the people of other nations.

This organization will differ from existing assistance programs in that its members will supplement technical advisers by offering the specific skills needed by developing nations if they are to put technical advice to work. They will help provide the skilled manpower necessary to carry out the development projects planned by the host governments, acting at a working level and serving at great personal sacrifice. There is little doubt that the number of those who wish to serve will be far greater than our capacity to absorb them.

The Peace Corps or some similar approach has been strongly advocated by Senator Humphrey, Representative

Reuss, and others in the Congress. It has received strong support from universities, voluntary agencies, student groups, labor unions, and business and professional organizations.

Last session, the Congress authorized a study of these possibilities. Preliminary reports of this study show that the Peace Corps is feasible, needed, and wanted by many foreign countries.

Most heartening of all, the initial reaction to this proposal has been an enthusiastic response by student groups, professional organizations, and private citizens everywhere—a convincing demonstration that we have in this country an immense reservoir of dedicated men and women willing to devote their energies and time and toil to the cause of world peace and human progress.

Among the specific programs to which Peace Corps members can contribute are: teaching in primary and secondary schools, especially as part of national English-language teaching programs; participation in the worldwide program of malaria eradication; instruction and operation of public health and sanitation projects; aiding in village development through school construction and other programs; increasing rural agricultural productivity by assisting local farmers to use modern implements and techniques. The initial emphasis of these programs will be on teaching. Thus the Peace Corps members will be an effective means of implementing the development programs of the host countries—programs which our technical assistance operations have helped to formulate.

The Peace Corps will not be limited to the young, or to college graduates. All Americans who are qualified will be welcome to join this effort. But undoubtedly the Corps will be made up primarily of young people as they complete their formal education.

Because one of the greatest resources of a free society is the strength and diversity of its private organizations and institutions much of the Peace Corps program will be carried out by these groups, financially assisted by the Federal Government.

Peace Corps personnel will be made available to developing nations in the following ways:

1. Through private voluntary agencies carrying on international assistance programs.

2. Through overseas programs of colleges and universities.

3. Through assistance programs of international agencies.

4. Through assistance programs of the United States government.

5. Through new programs which the Peace Corps itself directly administers.

In the majority of cases the Peace Corps will assume the entire responsibility for recruitment, training, and the development of overseas projects. In other cases it will make available a pool of trained applicants to private groups who are carrying out projects approved by the Peace Corps.

In the case of Peace Corps programs conducted through voluntary agencies and universities, these private institutions will have the option of using the national recruitment system—the central pool of trained manpower—or developing recruitment systems of their own.

In all cases men and women recruited as a result of Federal assistance will be members of the Peace Corps and enrolled in the central organization. All private recruitment and training programs will adhere to Peace Corps standards as a condition of Federal assistance.

In all instances the men and women of the Peace Corps will go only to those countries where their services and skills are genuinely needed and desired. U.S. Operations Missions, supplemented where necessary by special Peace Corps teams, will consult with leaders in foreign countries in order to determine where Peace Corpsmen are needed, the types of job they can best fill, and the number of people who can be usefully employed. The Peace Corps will not supply personnel for marginal undertakings without a sound economic or social justification. In furnishing assistance through the Peace Corps, careful regard will be given to the particular country's developmental priorities.

Membership in the Peace Corps will be open to all Americans, and applications will be available shortly. Where application is made directly to the Peace Corps—the vast majority of cases—they will be carefully screened to make sure that those who are selected can contribute to Peace Corps programs, and have the personal qualities which will enable them to represent the United States abroad with honor and dignity. In those cases where application is made directly to a private group, the same basic standards will be maintained. Each new recruit will receive a training and orientation period varying from six weeks to six months. This training will include courses in the culture and language of the country to which they are being sent and specialized training designed to increase the work skills of recruits. In some cases training will be conducted by participant agencies and universities in approved training programs. Other training programs will be conducted by the Peace Corps staff.

Length of service in the Corps will vary depending on the kind of project and the country, generally ranging from two to three years. Peace Corps members will often serve under conditions of physical hardship, living under primitive conditions among the people of developing nations. For every Peace Corps member service will mean a great financial sacrifice. They will receive no salary. Instead they will be

77

given an allowance which will only be sufficient to meet their basic needs and maintain health. It is essential that Peace Corpsmen and women live simply and unostentatiously among the people they have come to assist. At the conclusion of their tours, members of the Peace Corps will receive a small sum in the form of severance pay based on length of service abroad, to assist them during their first weeks back in the United States. Service with the Peace Corps will not exempt volunteers from Selective Service.

The United States will assume responsibility for supplying medical services to Peace Corps members and ensuring supplies and drugs necessary to good health.

I have asked the temporary Peace Corps to begin plans and make arrangements for pilot programs. A minimum of several hundred volunteers could be selected, trained, and at work abroad by the end of this calendar year. It is hoped that within a few years several thousand Peace Corps members will be working in foreign lands.

It is important to remember that this program must, in its early stages, be experimental in nature. This is a new dimension in our overseas program and only the most careful planning and negotiation can ensure its success.

The benefits of the Peace Corps will not be limited to the countries in which it serves. Our own young men and women will be enriched by the experience of living and working in foreign lands. They will have acquired new skills and experience which will aid them in their future careers and add to our own country's supply of trained personnel and teachers. They will return better able to assume the responsibilities of American citizenship and with greater understanding of our global responsibilities.

Although this is an American Peace Corps, the problem of world development is not just an American problem. Let us hope that other nations will mobilize the spirit and energies and skill of their people in some form of Peace Corps—making our own effort only one step in a major international effort to increase the welfare of all men and improve understanding among nations.

The response was overwhelming. The first Peace Corps volunteers were chosen, from 12,000 applicants. "The Peace Corps had captured the public imagination as had no other single act of the Kennedy Administration," said Time magazine of March 10.

Some of the recipient nations were hesitant because they feared that the Peace Corps volunteers might act as "tools of American propaganda" in their countries, but they were also hopeful—volunteers could answer some of the urgent needs which developing countries face.

By the beginning of September 1961 the first fifty volunteers were at work in their host countries, having undergone training in language, the government and customs of the host country, and physical training at the first Peace Corps training camp in Puerto Rico. The President addressed them before they departed for Ghana and Tanganyika, August 28, 1961:

I want to express my great pleasure at welcoming all of you who are the first members of the Peace Corps to be graduated from these schools and also the first members of the Peace Corps to be sent overseas.

Those of you who are going to Ghana to teach, I am sure that you realize how important and valuable is the work in which you are engaged. One of the great problems that the people of Africa face is the comparatively few experienced, educated leaders that they have for positions of responsibility during these first days of their independence.

I feel particular satisfaction because this is the most immediate response—the Peace Corps—that I think the

79

country has seen to the whole spirit I tried to suggest in my inaugural about the contributions which we can make to our country.

The fact that you've been willing to volunteer, that you've gone through very detailed, demanding tests, that you are willing to go to Ghana and Tanganyika, and other countries as time goes on—Americans who are without great compensation, all of you with special skills, which could mean that if you stayed home you could pursue your own private interests with a good deal of assurance of success—the fact that you are willing to do this for our country in the larger sense, as the name suggests, for the cause of peace and understanding, I think should make all Americans proud and make them all appreciative.

There are of course a great many hundreds of millions of people scattered throughout the world. You will come in contact with only a few, but the great impression of what kind of country we have and what kind of people we are will depend on their judgment, in these countries, of you. You will be the personification of a special group of young Americans, and if you can impress them with your commitment to freedom, to the advancement of the interests of people everywhere, to your pride in your country and its best traditions and what it stands for, the influence may be far-reaching and will go far beyond the immediate day-to-day tasks that you may do in the months that are ahead.

So I hope you realize—I know you do—that the future of the Peace Corps really rests with you. If you do well, then the Peace Corps will be developed and more and more Americans will go abroad and will find a greater and greater response to this idea of serving our country.

You're very welcome here, and we're all proud of you. And I must say, we put a good deal of hope in the work that you do.

In the face of cautious predictions of its achievement and success, the Peace Corps flourished. Volunteers were soon in more than forty countries, all at the request of the countries involved. Living with the people, sharing their poverty, their pleasures, and their problems, Peace Corps volunteers were soon building schools and roads, teaching subjects ranging from Latin and zoology to physical education and sewing, and showing that Americans could be anything but ugly. Although volunteers themselves often reported that they felt their contribution to the advancement of the people they were working with was small, almost all the countries have requested greater numbers of volunteers each year, indicating that the Corps' contribution is significant. And the idea of volunteer service has proved itself so effective that a domestic peace corps, the Volunteers in Service to America (VISTA), has been formed to assist our own underdeveloped regions.

In 1966, more than 14,000 volunteers were serving in forty-six countries. As nations all over the world asked for more help, and Americans willing to serve their country in the name of peace continued to come forward, President Johnson called for 20,000 volunteers by 1970. The continuing vigor and effectiveness of the Peace Corps remain one of President Kennedy's greatest contributions to the United States and to the world.

THE ARMED FORCES

●

No large military conflict took place during President Kennedy's administration. The Korean War had long been over, and American soldiers were serving in Vietnam only as military advisers to the Vietnamese troops, not as combatants. There were, however, two major confrontations with Russia. In 1961 the Russians threatened to end the international control of Berlin, and built a wall between East and West Berlin to prevent East Germans from fleeing to the west; U.S. troops were called up, and a crisis was averted. In October 1962, Russia was discovered to be building missile bases in Cuba; after Kennedy ordered a blockade to prevent shipments of military goods to the island, the Russians removed the bases, and war was narrowly averted. It was clear that a shooting war was avoided because of the existence of a thoroughly trained, well-equipped, and prepared military establishment.

President Kennedy's own military experience was gained in World War II, when he served in the Navy. In 1943 the PT boat he commanded was sunk in the South Pacific, and, despite a painful back injury, he towed an injured crewman to shore, then spent four days in the water searching for help before he and his crew were rescued. He received the Navy and Marine Corps Medal for heroism and leadership. He was well aware that in peace as well as in war, the nation's safety depends on the Armed Forces. He summed it up at the U.S. Naval Academy at Annapolis on August 1, 1963:

This country owes the greatest debt to our servicemen. In time of war, of course, there is a tremendous enthusiasm and outburst of popular feeling about those who fight and lead our wars, but it is sometimes different in peace. But I can assure the people of this country, from my own personal experience in the last two and a half years, that more than anything, more than anything, the fact that this country is secure and at peace, the fact that dozens of countries allied with us are free and at peace, has been due to the military strength of the United States. And that strength has been directly due to the men who serve in our Armed Forces. So even though it may be at peace, in fact most especially because it is at peace, I take this opportunity to express our appreciation to all of them whether they be here or whether they be out of sight of land, or beneath the sea.

The contributions of the Armed Forces are varied, and a great deal is expected of the men in service. The President spoke of their responsibilities to the nation at commencement exercises at the three military service academies. Most of the thoughts he addressed to the future officers apply as well to all members of the Army, Navy, Marines and Air Force.

Speech at U.S. Naval Academy, Annapolis, June 7, 1961

I am proud as a citizen of the United States to come to this institution and this room where there is concentrated so many men who have committed themselves to the defense of the United States. I am honored to be here.

In the past I have had some slight contact with this service, though I never did reach the state of professional and physical perfection where I could hope that anyone would ever mistake me for an Annapolis graduate.

I know that you are constantly warned during your days here not to mix, in your naval career, in politics. I should point out, however, on the other side, that my rather rapid rise from a reserve lieutenant, of uncertain standing, to Commander-in-Chief has been because I did not follow that very good advice.

I trust, however, that those of you who are Regulars will, for a moment, grant a retired civilian officer some measure of fellowship.

Nearly half a century ago, President Woodrow Wilson came here to Annapolis on a similar mission, and addressed the class of 1914. On that day, the graduating class numbered 154 men. There has been, since that time, a revolution in the size of our military establishment, and that revolution has been reflected in the revolution in the world around us.

When Wilson addressed the class of 1914, the Victorian structure of power was still intact, the world was dominated by Europe, and Europe itself was the scene of an uneasy balance of power between dominant figures and America was a spectator on a remote sideline.

The autumn after Wilson came to Annapolis, the Victorian world began to fall to pieces, and our world half a century later is vastly different. Today we are witnesses to the most extraordinary revolution, nearly, in the history of the world, as the emergent nations of Latin America, Africa, and Asia awaken from the long centuries of torpor and impatience.

Today the Victorian certitudes which were taken to be so much a part of man's natural existence are under siege by a faith committed to the destruction of liberal civilization, and today the United States is no longer the spectator, but the leader.

This half-century, therefore, has not only revolutionized the size of our military establishment, it has brought about also a more striking revolution in the things that the nation expects from the men in our Service.

Fifty years ago the graduates of the Naval Academy were expected to be seamen and leaders of men. They were reminded of the saying of John Paul Jones, "Give me a fair ship so that I might go into harm's way."

When Captain Mahan began to write in the nineties on the general issues of war and peace and naval strategy, the

85

Navy quickly shipped him to sea duty. Today we expect all of you—in fact, you must, of necessity—be prepared not only to handle a ship in a storm or a landing party on a beach, but to make great determinations which affect the survival of this country.

The revolution in the technology of war makes it necessary in order that you, when you hold positions of command, may make an educated judgment between various techniques, that you also be a scientist and an engineer and a physicist, and your responsibilities go far beyond the classic problems of tactics and strategy.

In the years to come, some of you will serve as your Commandant did last year, as an adviser to foreign governments; some will negotiate as Admiral Burke did, in Korea, with other governments on behalf of the United States; some will go to the far reaches of space and some will go to the bottom of the ocean. Many of you from one time or another, in the positions of command, or as members of staff, will participate in great decisions which go far beyond the narrow reaches of professional competence.

You gentlemen, therefore, have a most important responsibility, to recognize that your education is just beginning, and to be prepared, in the most difficult period in the life of our country, to play the role that the country hopes and needs and expects from you. You must understand not only this country but other countries. You must know something about strategy and tactics and logic—logistics, but also economics and politics and diplomacy and history. You must know everything you can about military power, and you must also understand the limits of military power. You must understand that few of the problems of our time have, in the final analysis, been finally solved by military power alone. When I say that officers today must go far beyond the official curriculum, I say it not because I do not believe in the traditional relationship between the civilian and the military, but you must be more than the servants of national policy. You must be prepared to play a construtive role in the development of national policy, a policy which protects our interests and our security and the peace of the world. Woodrow Wilson reminded your predecessors that you were not serving a government or an administration, but a people. In serving the American people, you represent the American people and the best of the ideals of this free society. Your posture and your performance will provide many people far beyond our shores, who know very little of our country, the only evidence they will ever see as to whether America is truly dedicated to the cause of justice and freedom.

In my inaugural address, I said that each citizen should be concerned not with what his country can do for him, but what he can do for his country. What you have chosen to do for your country, by devoting your life to the service of your country, is the greatest contribution that any man can make. It is easy for you, in a moment of exhilaration today, to say that you freely and gladly dedicate your life to the United States. But the life of service is a constant test of your will.

It will be hard at times to face the personal sacrifice and the family inconvenience, to maintain this high resolve, to place the needs of your country above all else. When there is a visible enemy to fight, the tide of patriotism in this country runs strong. But when there is a long, slow struggle, with no immediate visible foe, when you watch your contemporaries indulging the urge for material gain and comfort and personal advancement, your choice will seem hard, and you will recall, I am sure, the lines found in an old sentry box at Gibraltar, "God and the soldier all men adore in time of trouble and no more, for when war is over, and all things righted, God is neglected and the old soldier slighted."

Never forget, however, that the battle for freedom takes many forms. Those who through vigilance and firmness and devotion are the great servants of this country—and let us have no doubt that the United States needs your devoted assistance today.

The answer to those who callenge us so severely in so many parts of the globe lies in our willingness to freely commit ourselves to the maintenance of our country and the things for which it stands.

This ceremony today represents the kind of commitment which you are willing to make. For this reason, I am proud to be here. This nation salutes you as you commence your service to our country in the hazardous days ahead. And on behalf of all of them, I congratulate you and thank you.

Speech at U.S. Military Academy, West Point, June 6, 1962

I am sure that all of you who sit here today realize . . . that you are part of a long tradition stretching back to the earliest days of this country's history, and that where you sit sat once some of the most celebrated names in our nation's history, and also some who are not so well known, but who, on a hundred different battlefields in many wars involving every generation of this country's history, have given very clear evidence of their commitment to their country.

So that I know you feel a sense of pride at being a part of that tradition, and as a citizen of the United States, as well as President, I want to express our high regard to all of you in appreciation for what you are doing and what you will do for our country in the days ahead.

I want to say that I am sure you recognize that your schooling is only interrupted by today's occasion and not ended, because the demands that will be made upon you in the service of your country in the coming months and years will be really more pressing, and in many ways more burdensome, as well as more challenging, than ever before in our history. I know that many of you feel, and many of our citizens may feel that in these days of the nuclear age, when war may last in its final form a day or two or three days before much of the world is burned up, that your service to your country will be only standing and waiting. Nothing, of course, could be further from the truth. I am sure that many Americans believe that the days before World War II were the golden age when the stars were falling on all the graduates of West Point, that that was the golden time of service, and that you have moved into a period where military service, while vital, is not as challenging as it was then. Nothing could be further from the truth.

The fact of the matter is that the period just ahead in the next decade will offer more opportunities for service to the graduates of this academy than ever before in the history of the United States, because all around the world, in countries which are heavily engaged in the maintenance of their freedom, graduates of this academy are heavily involved. Whether it is in Vietnam or in Laos or in Thailand, whether it is a military advisory group in Iran, whether it is a military attaché in some Latin American country during a difficult and challenging period, whether it is the commander of our troops in South Korea—the burdens that will be placed upon you when you fill those positions, as you must inevitably, will require more from you than ever before in our history. The graduates of West Point, the Naval Academy, and the Air Academy in the next ten years will have the greatest opportunity for the defense of freedom

89

that this academy's graduates have ever had. And I am sure that the Joint Chiefs of Staff endorse that view, knowing as they do and I do, the heavy burdens that are required of this academy's graduates every day—General Tucker in Laos, or General Harkins in Vietnam, and a dozen others who hold key and significant positions involving the security of the United States and the defense of freedom. You are going to follow in their footsteps and I must say that I think that you will be privileged in the years ahead to find yourselves so heavily involved in the great interests of this country.

Therefore, I hope you realize—and I hope every American realizes—how much we depend upon you. Your strictly military responsibilities, therefore, will require a versatility and an adaptability never before required in either war or in peace. They may involve the command and control of modern nuclear weapons and modern delivery systems, so complex that only a few scientists can understand their operation, so devastating that their inadvertent use would be of worldwide concern, but so new that their employment and their effects have never been tested in combat conditions.

On the other hand, your responsibilities may involve the command of more traditional forces, but in less traditional roles—men risking their lives, not as combatants, but as instructors or advisers, or as symbols of our nation's commitment. The fact that the United States is not directly at war in these areas in no way diminishes the skill and courage that will be required, the service to our country which is rendered, or the pain of the casualties which are suffered.

To cite one final example of the range of responsibilities that will fall upon you: you may hold a position of command with our special forces, forces which are too unconventional to be called conventional, forces which are growing in number and importance and significance, for we now know that it is wholly misleading to call this "the nuclear age," or to say that our security rests only on the doctrine of massive retaliation.

Korea has not been the only battleground since the end of the Second World War. Men have fought and died in Malaya, in Greece, in the Philippines, in Algeria and Cuba and Cyprus, and almost continuously on the Indo-Chinese Peninsula. No nuclear weapons have been fired. No massive nuclear retaliation has been considered appropriate. This is another type of war, new in intensity, ancient in its origin— war by guerrillas, subversives, insurgents, assassins, war by ambush instead of by combat; by infiltration, instead of aggression, seeking victory by eroding and exhausting the enemy instead of engaging him. It is a form of warfare uniquely adapted to what has been strangely called "wars of liberation," to undermine the efforts of new and poor countries to maintain the freedom that they have finally achieved. It preys on economic unrest and ethnic conflicts. It requires in those situations where we must counter it, and these are the kinds of challenges that will be before us in the next decade if freedom is to be saved, a whole new kind of strategy, a wholly different kind of force, and therefore a new and wholly different kind of military training.

But I have spoken thus far only of the military challenges which your education must prepare you for. The nonmilitary problems which you will face will also be most demanding, diplomatic, political, and economic. In the years ahead, some of you will serve as advisers to foreign aid missions or even to foreign governments. Some will negotiate the terms of a cease-fire with broad political as well as military ramifications. Some of you will go to the far corners of the earth, and to the far reaches of space. Some of you will sit in the highest councils of the Pentagon. Others will hold delicate

91

command posts which are international in character. Still others will advise on plans to abolish arms instead of using them to abolish others. Whatever your position, the scope of your decisions will not be confined to the traditional tenets of military competence and training. You will need to know and understand not only the foreign policy of the United States but the foreign policy of all countries scattered around the world who twenty years ago were the most distant names to us. You will need to give orders in different tongues and read maps by different systems. You will be involved in economic judgments which most economists would hesitate to make. At what point, for example, does military aid become burdensome to a country and make its freedom endangered rather than helping to secure it? To what extent can the gold and dollar cost of your overseas deployments be offset by foreign procurements? Or at what stage can a new weapons system be considered sufficiently advanced to justify large dollar appropriations?

In many countries, your posture and performance will provide the local population with the only evidence of what our country is really like. In other countries, your military mission, its advice and action, will play a key role in determining whether those people will remain free. You will need to understand the importance of military power and also the limits of military power, to decide what arms should be used to fight and when they should be used to prevent a fight, to determine what represents our vital interests and what interests are only marginal.

Above all, you will have a responsibility to deter war as well as fight it. For the basic problems facing the world today are not susceptible of a final military solution. While we will long require the services and admire the dedication and commitment of the fighting men of this country, neither our strategy nor our psychology as a nation, and certainly

92

not our economy, must become permanently dependent upon an ever-increasing military establishment.

Our forces, therefore, must fulfill a broader role as a complement to our diplomacy, as an arm of our diplomacy, as a deterrent to our adversaries, and as a symbol to our allies of our determination to support them.

That is why this academy has seen its curriculum grow and expand in dimension, in substance, and in difficulty. That is why you cannot possibly have crowded into these four busy years all of the knowledge and all of the range of experience which you must bring to these subtle and delicate tasks which I have described. And that is why you will go to school year after year so that you can serve this country to the best of your military ability and your talent.

To talk of such talent and effort raises in the minds, I am sure, of everyone, and the minds of all of our countrymen, why—why should men such as you, able to master the complex arts of science, mathematics, language, economy, and all the rest devote their lives to a military career with all of its risks and hardships? Why should their families be expected to make the personal and financial sacrifices that a military career inevitably brings with it? When there is a visible enemy to fight in open combat, the answer is not so difficult. Many serve, all applaud, and the tide of patriotism runs high. But when there is a long, slow struggle, with no immediate visible foe, your choice will seem hard indeed. . . .

But you have one satisfaction, however difficult those days may be: when you are asked by a President of the United States or by any other American what you are doing for your country, no man's answer will be clearer than your own. And that moral motivation which brought you here in the first place is part of your training here as well. West Point was not built to produce technical experts alone. It was built to produce men committed to the defense of their

93

country, leaders of men who understand the great stakes which are involved, leaders who can be entrusted with the heavy responsibility which modern weapons and the fight for freedom entail, leaders who can inspire in their men the same sense of obligation to duty which you bring to it.

There is no single slogan that you can repeat to yourself in hard days or give to those who may be associated with you. In times past, a simple phrase, "54-40 or fight" or "to make the world safe for democracy"—that was enough. But the times, the weapons, and the issues are now more complicated than ever.

Eighteen years ago today, Ernie Pyle, describing those tens of thousands of young men who crossed the "ageless and indifferent" sea of the English Channel, searched in vain for a word to describe what they were fighting for. And finally he concluded that they were at least fighting for each other.

You and I leave here today to meet our separate responsibilities, to protect our nation's vital interests by peaceful means if possible, by resolute action if necessary. And we go forth confident of support and success because we know that we are working and fighting for each other and for all those men and women all over the globe who are determined to be free.

Speech at U.S. Air Force Academy, Colorado Springs, June 5, 1963

It is customary for speakers on these occasions to say in graduating addresses that commencement signifies the beginning instead of the end, yet this thought applies with particular force to those of you who are graduating from our nation's Service academies today, for today you receive not only your degrees, but also your commissions, and tomorrow you join with all those in the military service, in the foreign service, the civil service, and elsewhere, and one million of them serve outside our frontiers who have chosen to serve the great Republic at a turning point in our history. You will have an opportunity to help make that history—an opportunity for a Service career more varied and demanding than any that has been opened to any officer corps in the history of any country.

There are some who might be sceptical of that assertion. They claim that the future of the Air Force is mortgaged to an obsolete weapons system, the manned aircraft, or that the Air Force officers of the future will be nothing more than "silent silo sitters," but nothing could be further from the truth. It is this very onrush of technology which demands an expanding role for the nation's Air Force and Air Force officers, and which guarantees that an Air Force career in the next forty years will be even more changing and more challenging than the careers of the last forty years.

For some of you will travel where no man has ever traveled before. Some of you will fly the fastest planes that have ever been built, reach the highest altitudes that man has ever gone to, and lift the heaviest payloads of any aviator in history. Some of you will hold in your hands the most awesome destructive power which any nation or any man has conceived. Some of you will work with the leaders of new nations which were not even nations a few years ago. Some of you will support guerrilla and counter-guerrilla operations that combine the newest techniques of warfare with the oldest techniques of the jungle, and some of you will help develop new planes that spread their wings in flight, detect other planes at an unheard-of distance, deliver new weapons with unprecedented accuracy, and survey the ground from incredible heights as a testament to our

95

strong faith in the future of air power and the manned airplane. . . .

The fact that the greatest value of all of the weapons of massive retaliation lies in their ability to deter war does not diminish their importance, nor will national security in the years ahead be achieved simply by piling up bigger bombs or burying our missiles under bigger loads of concrete. For in an imperfect world where human folly has been the rule and not the exception, the surest way to bring on the war that can never happen is to sit back and assure ourselves it will not happen. The existence of mutual nuclear deterrents cannot be shrugged off as stalemate, for our national security in a period of rapid change will depend on constant reappraisal of our present doctrines, on alertness to new developments, on imagination and resourcefulness, and new ideas. Stalemate is a static term and not one of you would be here today if you believed you were entering an outmoded service requiring only custodial duties in a period of nuclear stalemate. . . .

The Air Force officer of today and tomorrow requires the broadest kind of scholarship to understand a most complex and changing world. He requires understanding and learning unmatched in the days before World War II. Any graduate of this academy who serves in our Armed Forces will need to know economics and history, and international affairs, and languages. You will need an appreciation of other societies, and an understanding of our own nation's purposes and policy. . . .

Last October's crisis in the Caribbean amply demonstrated that military power and policy cannot and must not be separated from political and diplomatic decisions. Whatever the military motive and implications of the reckless attempt to put missiles on the island of Cuba, the political and psychological implications were equally important. We needed in October—and we had them and we shall need them in the future, and we shall have them—military commanders who are conscious of the enormous stakes in the nuclear age of every decision that they take, who are aware of the fact that there are no purely political decisions or purely military decisions; that every problem is a mixture of both, men who know the difference between vital interests and peripheral interests, who can maneuver military forces with precision and judgment, as well as courage and determination, and who can foresee the effects of military action on political policy. We need men, in short, who can cope with the challenges of a new political struggle, an armed doctrine which uses every weapon in the struggle around the globe.

We live in a world, in short, where the principal problems that we face are not susceptible to military solutions alone. The role of our military power, in essence, is, therefore, to free ourselves and our allies to pursue the goals of freedom without the danger of enemy attack, but we do not have a separate military policy, and a separate diplomatic policy, and a separate disarmament policy, and a separate foreign aid policy, all unrelated to each other. They are all bound up together in the policy of the United States. Our goal is a coherent, overall, national security policy, one that truly serves the best interests of this country and those who depend on it. It is worth noting that all of the decisions which we now face today will come in increased numbers in the months and years ahead.

I want to congratulate all of you who have chosen the United States Air Force as a career. As far as any of us can now see in Washington in the days ahead, you will occupy positions of the highest responsibility, and merely because we move into a period of change in weapon technology, as well as political challenge, because, in fact, we move into that period, there is greater need for you than ever before. You, here today on this field, your colleagues at Omaha, Nebraska, or at Elgin in Florida, or who may be stationed in Western Europe, or men who are at sea in ships hundreds of miles from land, or soldiers in camps in Texas or on the island of Okinawa, they maintain the freedom by being on the ready. They maintain the freedom, the security, and the peace not only of the United States, but of all the dozens of countries who are allied to us who are close to the Communist power and who depend upon us and, in a sense, only upon us for their freedom and security. These distant ships, these distant planes, these distant men keep the peace in a great half-circle stretching all the way from Berlin to South Korea. This is the role which history and our own determination has placed upon a country which lived most of its history in isolation and neutrality, and yet in the last eighteen years has carried the burden for free people everywhere. I think that this is a burden which we accept willingly, recognizing that if this country does not accept it, no people will, recognizing that in the most difficult time in the whole life of freedom, the United States is called upon to play its greatest role. This is a role which we are proud to accept, and I am particularly proud to see the United States accept it in the presence of these young men who have committed themselves to the service of our country and to the cause of its freedom.

CIVIL RIGHTS

●

The movement for Negro equality had grown in the 1950's
to become the number-one domestic issue in Kennedy's administration. Demonstrations and resistance increased tensions,
particularly in the South, to the point of violence. In 1961,
Attorney General Robert F. Kennedy was compelled to send

United States marshals to Montgomery, Alabama, when rioting broke out against a group of freedom riders. The continued reluctance of public authorities to abide by court decisions in favor of integration continued to provoke crises. In 1962 the President ordered 3,000 federal troops to the campus of the University of Mississippi to quell riots that took place when a Negro, James Meredith, attempted to register at the university. He employed Federal troops twice in 1963, to enforce the integration of the University of Alabama and of the public schools in three Alabama cities against opposition from Governor George Wallace.

President Kennedy's concern was not just to avert violence. He was determined to make laws that would back up the constitutional guarantee of equal rights for all. He presented a bill to Congress that would require public places, like restaurants and hotels, to accept customers regardless of race. He also asked that the Attorney General be allowed to bring suit in behalf of private citizens to desegregate schools. The Congress passed a modified version of Kennedy's bill in 1964.

Kennedy also did much to promote equality in the government. When an investigation revealed that shockingly few Negroes were employed by the government, especially in the higher ranks, the President demanded immediate improvement. Between June 1961 and June 1963, the number of Negroes in the middle civil-service grades increased 36.6%, and in the top grades 88.2%. The President also appointed a number of Negroes to prominent positions. Included were Robert C. Weaver as head of the Housing Administration, George Weaver as Assistant Secretary of Labor, Carl Rowan as Deputy Assistant Secretary of State for Public Affairs, Clifton R. Wharton as Ambassador to Norway, Thurgood Marshall as judge on the Third Circuit Court.

In two addresses to the American people, President Kennedy spelled out what every citizen must do in a time of

100

struggle over civil rights. The first address was made on September 30, 1962, after Meredith's attempt to register at the University of Mississippi had been defied by Governor Ross Barnett; the second came when the integration crisis developed at the University of Alabama, June 11, 1963.

Our nation is founded on the principle that observance of the law is the eternal safeguard of liberty and defiance of the law is the surest road to tyranny. The law which we obey includes the final rulings of the courts, as well as the enactments of our legislative bodies. Even among law-abiding men few laws are universally loved, but they are uniformly respected and not resisted.

Americans are free, in short, to disagree with the law but not to disobey it. For in a government of laws and not of men, no man, however prominent or powerful, and no mob, however unruly or boisterous, is entitled to defy a court of law. If this country should ever reach the point where any man or group of men by force or threat of force could long defy the commands of our court and our Constitution, then no law would stand free from doubt, no judge would be sure of his writ, and no citizen would be safe from his neighbors. . . .

This nation is proud of the many instances in which governors, educators, and everyday citizens from the South have shown to the world the gains that can be made by persuasion and good will in a society ruled by law. Specifically, I would like to take this occasion to express the thanks of this nation to those southerners who have contributed to the progress of our democratic development in the entrance of students regardless of race to such great institutions as the state-supported universities of Virginia, North Carolina, Georgia, Florida, Texas, Louisiana, Tennessee, Arkansas, and Kentucky. . . .

101

You have a new opportunity to show that you are men of patriotism and integrity. For the most effective means of upholding the law is not the state policeman or the marshals or the National Guard. It is you. It lies in your courage to accept those laws with which you disagree as well as those with which you agree. The eyes of the nation and of all the world are upon you and upon all of us, and the honor of your university and state are in the balance. I am certain that the great majority of the students will uphold that honor. . . .

Let us preserve both the law and the peace and then healing those wounds that are within we can turn to the greater crises that are without and stand united as one people in our pledge to man's freedom.

This nation was founded by men of many nations and backgrounds. It was founded on the principle that all men are created equal, and that the rights of every man are diminished when the rights of one man are threatened.

Today we are committed to a worldwide struggle to promote and protect the rights of all who wish to be free. And when Americans are sent to Vietnam or West Berlin, we do not ask for whites only. It ought to be possible, therefore, for American students of any color to attend any public institution they select without having to be backed up by troops.

It ought to be possible for American consumers of any color to receive equal service in places of public accommodation, such as hotels and restaurants and theaters and retail stores, without being forced to resort to demonstrations in the street, and it ought to be possible for American citizens of any color to register and to vote in a free election without interference or fear of reprisal.

It ought to be possible, in short, for every American to

enjoy the privileges of being American without regard to his race or his color. In short, every American ought to have the right to be treated as he would wish to be treated, as one would wish his children to be treated. But this is not the case.

The Negro baby born in America today, regardless of the section of the nation in which he is born, has about one-half as much chance of completing a high school as a white baby born in the same place on the same day, one-third as much chance of completing college, one-third as much chance of becoming a professional man, twice as much chance of becoming unemployed, about one-seventh as much chance of earning $10,000 a year, a life expectancy which is seven years shorter, and the prospects of earning only half as much.

This is not a sectional issue. Difficulties over segregation and discrimination exist in every city, in every state of the Union, producing in many cities a rising tide of discontent that threatens the public safety. Nor is this a partisan issue. In a time of domestic crisis men of good will and generosity should be able to unite regardless of party or politics. This is not even a legal or legislative issue alone. It is better to settle these matters in the courts than on the streets, and new laws are needed at every level, but law alone cannot make men see right.

We are confronted primarily with a moral issue. It is as old as the scriptures and is as clear as the American Constitution.

The heart of the question is whether all Americans are to be afforded equal rights and equal opportunities, whether we are going to treat our fellow Americans as we want to be treated. If an American, because his skin is dark, cannot eat lunch in a restaurant open to the public, if he cannot send his children to the best public school available, if he

103

cannot vote for the public officials who represent him, if, in short, he cannot enjoy the full and free life which all of us want, then who among us would be content to have the color of his skin changed and stand in his place? Who among us would then be content with the counsels of patience and delay?

One hundred years of delay have passed since President Lincoln freed the slaves, yet their heirs, their grandsons, are not fully free. They are not yet freed from the bonds of injustice. They are not yet freed from social and economic oppression. And this nation, for all its hopes and all its boasts, will not be fully free until all its citizens are free.

We preach freedom around the world, and we mean it, and we cherish our freedom here at home, but are we to say to the world, and much more importantly, to each other, that this is a land of the free except for the Negroes; that we have no second-class citizens except Negroes; that we have no class or caste system, no ghettoes, no master race except with respect to Negroes?

Now the time has come for this nation to fulfill its promise. The events in Birmingham and elsewhere have so increased the cries for equality that no city or state or legislative body can prudently choose to ignore them.

The fires of frustration and discord are burning in every city, North and South, where legal remedies are not at hand. Redress is sought in the streets, in demonstrations, parades, and protests which create tensions and threaten violence and threaten lives.

We face, therefore, a moral crisis as a country and as a people. It cannot be met by repressive police action. It cannot be left to increased demonstrations in the streets. It cannot be quieted by token moves or talk. It is a time to act in the Congress, in your state and local legislative body and, above all, in all of our daily lives.

It is not enough to pin the blame on others, to say this is a problem of one section of the country or another, or deplore the fact that we face. A great change is at hand, and our task, our obligation, is to make that revolution, that change, peaceful and constructive for all.

Those who do nothing are inviting shame as well as violence. Those who act boldly are recognizing right as well as reality. . . .

But legislation, I repeat, cannot solve this problem alone. It must be solved in the homes of every American in every community across our country.

In this respect, I want to pay tribute to those citizens North and South who have been working in their communities to make life better for all. They are acting not out of a sense of legal duty but out of a sense of human decency.

Like our soldiers and sailors in all parts of the world they are meeting freedom's challenge on the firing line, and I salute them for their honor and their courage.

My fellow Americans, this is a problem which faces us all—in every city of the North as well as the South. Today there are Negroes unemployed, two or three times as many compared to whites, inadequate in education, moving into the large cities, unable to find work, young people particularly out of work without hope, denied equal rights, denied the opportunity to eat at a restaurant or lunch counter or go to a movie theater, denied the right to a decent education, denied almost today the right to attend a state university even though qualified. It seems to me that these are matters which concern us all, not merely Presidents or congressmen or governors, but every citizen of the United States.

This is one country. It has become one country because all of us and all the people who came here had an equal chance to develop their talents.

We cannot say to 10 percent of the population that you can't have that right; that your children can't have the chance to develop whatever talents they have; that the only way that they are going to get their rights is to go into the streets and demonstrate. I think we owe them and we owe ourselves a better country than that.

Therefore, I am asking for your help in making it easier for us to move ahead and to provide the kind of equality of treatment which we would want ourselves; to give a chance for every child to be educated to the limit of his talents.

As I have said before, not every child has an equal talent or an equal ability or an equal motivation, but they should have the equal right to develop their talent and their ability and their motivation, to make something of themselves.

We have a right to expect that the Negro community will be responsible, will uphold the law, but they have a right to expect that the law will be fair, that the Constitution will be color-blind, as Justice Harlan said at the turn of the century.

This is what we are talking about and this is a matter which concerns this country and what it stands for, and in meeting it I ask the support of all our citizens.

CONSERVATION

●

The conservation of America's resources—both areas of untouched natural beauty for recreation and important natural resources like air, water, coal, and minerals for human and industrial consumption—was becoming an increasingly important issue when Kennedy took office. The new President had campaigned vigorously for a Cape Cod National Seashore when he was a Senator, and he was extremely pleased to sign the bill creating it officially. The project was particularly close to his heart because of his own love for the sea and the coastlands, where he had spent so many happy vacations. On numerous other nature conservation projects he backed his strong, outspoken Secretary of the Interior, Stewart Udall.

But the problem of conserving areas of great natural beauty was only part of a wider concern for the efficient use of all natural resources. Resources must be used in such a way as not to ruin them for the future. There is also need to find new resources, using what we have to develop more. Kennedy's thoughts on the use of our natural resources are set forth below.

Dedication Speech, National Wildlife Federation Building, March 3, 1961

At the inauguration, Robert Frost read a poem which began "the land was ours before we were the land's"—meaning, in part, that this new land of ours sustained us before we were a nation. And although we are now the land's— a nation of people matched to a continent—we still draw our strength and sustenance in every . . . city across our country from the earth.

Throughout our history our soil and water, our forests and minerals, have provided the resources upon which this country grew—and our power ascended. Today, this great gift of material wealth provides the foundation upon which the defense of freedom rests, here and around the world. And our future greatness and our strength depend upon the continued abundant use of our natural resources.

Thus it is our task in our time and in our generation to hand down undiminished to those who come after us, as was handed down to us by those who went before, the natural wealth and beauty which is ours. To do this will require constant attention and vigilance—sustained vigor and imagination.

No governmental program will be effective—our resources will not be protected—without the concern and help of every private citizen. By mobilizing private effort through this organization you are helping not only to develop the wildlife resources of our country—but you are helping to create the kind of America that is our common goal: an America of open spaces, of fresh water, of green country—a place where wildlife and natural beauty cannot be despoiled—where an increasingly urbanized population can still go to the country, can still turn back the clock of our civilization and find the material and spiritual strength upon which our greatness as a country depends.

More than one hundred years ago, a Senator from the East, speaking with prophecy, as Senators from the East frequently do, said that "to talk about constructing a railroad to the western shores of this continent manifests a spirit of wild adventure which I never expected to hear broached in the Senate of the United States." But that spirit prevailed—and this country grew—and that railroad went West. Today we once again call upon that "spirit of wild adventure"—and once again act to develop those resources which lie beneath our earth, in our mountains, in our rivers—and lie most of all in our people.

Speech at the University of Wyoming, September 25, 1963

This country has become rich because nature was good to us, and because the people who came from Europe, predominantly, also were among the most vigorous. The basic resources were used skillfully and economically, and because of the wise work done by Theodore Roosevelt and others, significant progress was made in conserving these resources.

The problem, of course, now is that the whole concept of conservation must change in the 1960's if we are going to pass on to the 350 million Americans who will live in this country in forty years where 180 million Americans now live—if we are going to pass on a country which is even richer.

The fact of the matter is that the management of our natural resources instead of being primarily a problem of conserving them, of saving them, now requires the scientific application of knowledge to develop new resources. We have come to realize to a large extent that resources are not passive. Resources are not merely something that was here, put by nature. Research tells us that previously valueless materials, which ten years ago were useless, now can be among the most valuable resources of the United States. And that is the most significant fact in conservation now since the early 1900's when Theodore Roosevelt started his work. A conservationist's first reaction in those day was to preserve, to hoard, to protect every non-renewable resource. It was the fear of resource exhaustion which caused the great conservation movement of the 1900's. And this fear was reflected in the speeches and attitudes of our political leaders and their writers.

This is not surprising in the light of the technology of that time, but today that approach is out of date, and I think this is an important fact. It is both too pessimistic and too optimistic. We need no longer fear that our resources and energy supplies are a fixed quantity that can be exhausted in accordance with a particular rate of consumption. On the other hand, it is not enough to put barbed wire around a forest or lake, or put in stockpiles of minerals, or restrictive laws and regulations on the exploitation of resources. That was the old way of doing it.

Our primary task now is to increase our understanding of our environment to a point where we can enjoy it without defacing it, use its bounty without detracting permanently from its value, and, above all, maintain a living balance between man's actions and nature's reactions, for this nation's great resources are as elastic and productive as our ingenuity can make them. Take, for example, soda ash which is a multimillion dollar industry in this state. A few years ago there was no use for it. It was wasted. People were unaware of it. And even if it had been sought, it could not be found—not because it wasn't here, but because effective prospecting techniques had not yet been developed. Now soda ash is a necessary ingredient in the production of glass, steel, and other products. As a result of a series of experiments, of a harnessing of science to the use of man, this great new industry has opened up. In short, conservation is no longer protection and conserving and restricting. The balance between our needs and the availability of our resources, between our aspirations and our environment, is constantly changing.

One of the great resources which we are going to find in the next forty years is not going to be the land; it will be the ocean. We are going to find untold wealth in the oceans of the world which will be used to make a better life for our people. Science is changing all of our natural environment.

It can change it for good; it can change it for bad. We are pursuing, for example, new opportunities for coal, which have been largely neglected—examining the feasibility of transporting coal by water through pipelines, of gasification at the mines, of liquefaction of coal into gasoline, and of transmitting electric power directly from the mouth of the mine. The economic feasibility of some of these techniques has not been determined, but it will be in the next decade. At the same time, we are engaged in active research on better means of using low-grade coal to meet the tremendous increase in the demand for coal we are going to find in the rest of this century. This is, in effect, using science to increase our supply of a resource of which the people of the United States were totally unaware fifty years ago.

Another research undertaking of special concern to this nation is the continuing effort to develop practical and feasible techniques of converting oil shale into usable petroleum fuels. The higher-grade deposits in Wyoming alone are equivalent to 30 billion barrels of oil, and 200 billion barrels in the case of lower-grade development. This could not be used, there was nothing to conserve, and now science is going to make it possible.

Investigation is going on at the same time to assure an adequate water supply so that when we develop this great new industry we will be able to use it and have sufficient water. Resource development, therefore, requires not only the coordination of all branches of science, it requires the joint effort of scientists, government—state, national, and local—and members of other professional disciplines. For example, we are now examining in the United States today the mixed economic-technical question of whether very large-scale nuclear reactors can produce unexpected savings in the simultaneous desalinization of water and the generation of electricity. We will have, before this decade is out or sooner, a tremendous nuclear reactor which makes electricity and at the same time gets fresh water from salt water at a competitive price. What a difference this can make to the western United States. And, indeed, not only the United States, but all around the globe where there are so many deserts on the ocean's edge. . . .

In 1970, 1980, 1990, this country will be, can be, must be—if we make the proper decisions, if we manage our resources, both human and material, wisely, if we make wise decisions in the nation, in the state, in the community, and individually, if we maintain a vigorous and hopeful pursuit of life and knowledge—the resources of this country are so unlimited and science is expanding them so greatly that all those people who thought forty years ago that this country would be exhausted in the middle of the century have been proven wrong. It is going to be richer than ever, providing we make the wise decisions and we recognize that the future belongs to those who seize it.

113

THE UNITED STATES
AND WORLD AFFAIRS

●

The keynote of President Kennedy's approach to international relations was to "make the world safe for diversity." Through years of fluctuating world tensions he met crises with firmness (in Berlin, Cuba, and other trouble spots), but he also concentrated on devising ways to lessen tensions, to open new pathways of understanding, and to enable the world to live in security from the fear of destruction, no matter what political beliefs are involved. Wholly committed to democracy and the freedom of the individual, he sought ways to encourage self-determination and development of peoples throughout the world. He felt that the United States, as the world's most powerful and highly developed nation, has a responsibility to help less fortunate nations and to use its power to the greatest extent possible to promote peace and prosperity. Foreign aid and the Peace Corps, sales of wheat to Russia and attempts to reduce international tariff barriers, all are designed in one way or another toward increasing communications with other countries and fulfilling our obligations to them and to ourselves.

He explained the need to keep up and expand our international commitments in an address at the Mormon Tabernacle in Salt Lake City, Utah, on September 26, 1963:

I want to speak about the responsibility that I feel the United States has not in this country, but abroad, and I see the closest interrelationship between the strength of the United States here as home and the strength of the United States around the world. . . .

What happens here in this country affects the security of the United States and the cause of freedom around the globe. If this is a strong, vital, and vigorous society, the cause of freedom will be strong and vital and vigorous.

I know that many of you sometimes wonder where we are going and why the United States should be so involved in so many affairs, in so many countries all around the globe. If our task on occasion seems hopeless, if we despair of ever working our will on the other 94 percent of the world population, then let us remember that the Mormons of a century ago were a persecuted and prosecuted minority, harried from place to place, the victims of violence and occasionally murder, while today, in the short space of 100 years, their faith and works are known and respected the world around, and their voices heard in the highest councils of this country.

As the Mormons succeeded, so America can succeed, if we will not give up or turn back. I realize that the burdens are heavy and I realize that there is a great tempation to urge that we relinquish them, that we have enough to do here in the United States, and we should not be so busy around the globe. The fact of the matter is that we, this generation of Americans, are the first generation of our country ever to be involved in affairs around the globe. From the beginning of this country, from the days of Washington, until the Second World War, this country lived an isolated existence. Through most of our history we were an unaligned country, an uncommitted nation, a neutralist nation. We were by statute as well as by desire. We had believed that we could live behind our two oceans in safety and prosperity in a comfortable distance from the rest of the world.

The end of isolation consequently meant a wrench with the very lifeblood, the very spine, of the nation. Yet, as time passed, we came to see that the end of isolation was not such a terrible error or evil after all. We came to see that it was the inevitable result of growth, the economic growth, the military growth, and the cultural growth of the United States. No nation so powerful and so dynamic and as rich as our own could hope to live in isolation from other nations, especially at a time when science and technology was making the world so small. . . .

We did not seek to become a world power. This position was thrust upon us by events. But we became one just the same, and I am proud that we did.

I can well understand the attraction of those earlier days.

116

Each one of us has moments of longing for the past, but two world wars have clearly shown us, try as we may, that we cannot turn our back on the world outside. If we do, we jeopardize our economic well-being, we jeopardize our political stability, we jeopardize our physical safety.

To turn away now is to abandon the world to those whose ambition is to destroy a free society. To yield these burdens up after having carried them for more than twenty years is to surrender the freedom of our country inevitably, for without the United States, the chances of freedom surviving, let alone prevailing around the globe, are nonexistent.

Americans have come a long way in accepting in a short time the necessity of world involvement, but the strain of this involvement remains and we find it all over the country. I see it in the letters that come to my desk every day. We find ourselves entangled with apparently unanswerable problems in unpronounceable places. We discover that our enemy in one decade is our ally the next. We find ourselves committed to governments whose actions we cannot often approve, assisting societies with principles very different from our own.

The burdens of maintaining an immense military establishment with one million Americans serving outside our frontiers, of financing a far-flung program of development assistance, of conducting a complex and baffling diplomacy, all weigh heavily upon us and cause some to counsel retreat. The world is full of contradiction and confusion, and our policy seems to have lost the black and white clarity of simpler times when we remembered the Maine and went to war.

It is little wonder, then, in this confusion, we look back to the old days with nostalgia. It is little wonder that there is a desire in the country to go back to the time when our nation lived alone. It is little wonder that we increasingly want an

117

end to entangling alliances, an end to all help to foreign countries, a cessation of diplomatic relations with countries or states whose principles we dislike, that we get the United Nations out of the United States, and the United States out of the United Nations, and that we retreat to our own hemisphere, or even within our own boundaries, to take refuge behind a wall of force.

This is an understandable effort to recover an old feeling of simplicity, yet in world affairs, as in all other aspects of our lives, the days of the quiet past are gone forever. Science and technology are irreversible. We cannot return to the day of the sailing schooner or the covered wagon, even if we wished. And if this nation is to survive and succeed in the real world of today, we must acknowledge the realities of the world; and it is those realities that I mention now.

We must first of all recognize that we cannot remake the world simply by our own command. When we cannot even bring all of our own people into full citizenship without acts of violence, we can understand how much harder it is to control events beyond our borders.

Every nation has its own traditions, its own values, its own aspirations. Our assistance from time to time can help other nations preserve their independence and advance their growth, but we cannot remake them in our own image. We cannot enact their laws, nor can we operate their governments or dictate their policies.

Second, we must recognize that every nation determines its policies in terms of its own interests. "No nation," George Washington wrote, "is to be trusted farther than it is bound by its interest; and no prudent statesman or politician will depart from it." National interest is more powerful than ideology, and the recent developments within the Communist empire show this very clearly. Friendship, as Palmerston said, may rise or wane, but interests endure.

118

The United States has rightly determined, in the years since 1945 under three different administrations, that our interest, our national security, the interest of the United States of America, is best served by preserving and protecting a world of diversity in which no one power or no one combination of powers can threaten the security of the United States. The reason that we moved so far into the world was our fear that at the end of the war, and particularly when China became Communist, that Japan and Germany would collapse, and these two countries which had so long served as a barrier to the Soviet advance, and the Russian advance before that, would open up a wave of conquest of all of Europe and all of Asia, and then the balance of power turning against us we would finally be isolated and ultimately destroyed. That is what we have been engaged in for eighteen years, to prevent that happening, to prevent any one monolithic power having sufficient force to destroy the United States.

For that reason we support the alliances in Latin America; for that reason we support NATO to protect the security of Western Europe; for that reason we joined SEATO to protect the security of Asia—so that neither Russia nor China could control Europe and Asia, and if they could not control Europe and Asia, then our security was assured. This is what we have been involved in doing. And however dangerous and hazardous it may be, and however close it may take us to the brink on occasion, which it has, and however tired we may get of our involvements with these governments so far away, we have one simple central theme of American foreign policy which all of us must recognize, because it is a policy which we must continue to follow, and that is to support the independence of nations so that one block cannot gain sufficient power to finally overcome us. There is no mistaking the vital interest of the United States

119

in what goes on around the world. Therefore, accepting what George Washington said here, I realize that what George Washington said about no entangling alliances has been ended by science and technology and danger.

And third, we must recognize that foreign policy in the modern world does not lend itself to easy, simple black and white solution. If we were to have diplomatic relations only with those countries whose principles we approved of, we would have relations with very few countries in a very short time. If we were to withdraw our assistance from all governments who are run differently from our own, we would relinquish half the world immediately to our adversaries. If we were to treat foreign policy as merely a medium for delivering self-righteous sermons to supposedly inferior people, we would give up all thought of world influence or world leadership.

For the purpose of foreign policy is not to provide an outlet for our own sentiments of hope or indignation; it is to shape real events in a real world. We cannot adopt a policy which says that if something does not happen, or others do not do exactly what we wish, we will return to "Fortress America." That is the policy in this changing world of retreat, not of strength.

More important, to adopt a black or white, all or nothing policy subordinates our interest to our irritations. Its actual consequences would be fatal to our security. If we were to resign from the United Nations, break off with all countries of whom we disapprove, end foreign aid and assistance to those countries in an attempt to keep them free, call for the resumption of atmospheric nuclear testing, and turn our back on the rest of mankind, we would not only be abandoning America's influence in the world, we would be inviting a Communist expansion which every Communist power would so greatly welcome. And all of the effort of so many

Americans for eighteen years would be gone with the wind. Our policy under those conditions, in this dangerous world, would not have much deterrent effect in a world where nations determined to be free could no longer count on the United States.

Such a policy of retreat would be folly if we had our backs to the wall. It is surely even greater folly at a time when more realistic, more responsible, more affirmative policies have wrought such spectacular results. For the most striking thing about our world [today] is the extent to which the tide of history has begun to flow in the direction of freedom. To renounce the world of freedom now, to abandon those who share our commitment, and retire into lonely and not so splendid isolation, would be to give Communism the one hope which, in this twilight of disappointment for them, might repair their divisions and rekindle their hope.

For after some gains in the fifties the Communist offensive, which claimed to be riding the tide of historic inevitability, has been thwarted and turned back in recent months. Indeed, the whole theory of historical inevitability, the belief that all roads must lead to Communism, sooner or later, has been shattered by the determination of those who believe that men and nations will pursue a variety of roads, that each nation will evolve according to its own traditions and its own aspirations, and that the world of the future will have room for a diversity of economic systems, political creeds, religious faiths, united by the respect for others, and loyalty to a world order.

Those forces of diversity which served Mr. Washington's national interest—those forces of diversity are in the ascendancy today, even within the Communist empire itself. And our policy at this point should be to give the forces of diversity, as opposed to the forces of uniformity, which our

121

adversaries espouse, every chance, every possible support. That is why our assistance program, so much maligned, of assisting countries to maintain their freedom, I believe, is important.

This country has seen all of the hardship and the grief that has come to us by the loss of one country in this hemisphere, Cuba. How many other countries must be lost if the United States decides to end the programs that are helping these people, who are getting poorer every year, who have none of the resources of this great country, who look to us for help, but on the other hand in cases look to the Communists for example?

That is why I think this program is important. It is a means of assisting those who want to be free, and in the final analysis it serves the United States in a very real sense. That is why the United Nations is important, not because it can solve all these problems in this imperfect world, but it does give us a means, in those great moments of crisis, and in the last two and a half years we have had at least three, when the Soviet Union and the United States were almost face to face on a collision course . . . it does give a means to mobilize the opinion of the world to prevent an atomic disaster which would destroy us all wherever we might live.

That is why the test ban treaty is important as a first step, perhaps to be disappointed, perhaps to find ourselves ultimately set back, but at least in 1963 the United States committed itself, and the Senate of the United States, by an overwhelming vote, to one chance to end the radiation and the possibilities of burning.

It may be, as I said, that we may fail, but anyone who bothers to look at the true destructive power of the atom today and what we and the Soviet Union could do to each other and the world in an hour and in a day, and to Western Europe—I passed over yesterday the Little Big Horn where

General Custer was slain, a massacre which has lived in history, 400 or 500 men. We are talking about 300 million men and women in twenty-four hours.

I think it is wise to take a first step to lessen the possibility of that happening. And that is why our diplomacy is important. For the forces making for diversity are to be found everywhere people are, even within the Communist empire, and it is our obligation to encourage those forces wherever they may be found. Hard and discouraging questions remain in Vietnam, in Cuba, in Laos, the Congo, all around the globe. The ordeal of the emerging nations has just begun. The control of nuclear weapons is still incomplete. The areas of potential friction, the chances of collision, still exist.

But in every one of these areas the position of the United States, I believe, is happier and safer when history is going for us rather than when it is going against us. And we have history going for us today, but history is what men make it. The future is what men make it.

We cannot fulfill our vision and our commitment and our interest in a free and diverse future without unceasing vigilance, devotion, and, most of all, perseverance, a willingness to do with fatigue, a willingness not to accept easy answers, but instead, to maintain the burden, as the people of this state have done for 100 years, and as the United States must do the rest of this century until finally we live in a peaceful world.

Therefore, I think this country will continue its commitments to support the world of freedom, for as we discharge that commitment we are heeding the command which Brigham Young heard from the Lord more than a century ago, the command he conveyed to his followers, "Go as pioneers . . . to a land of peace."

One of the most crucial and far-reaching programs initiated by President Kennedy was the Alliance for Progress (*Alianza para el Progreso*), a ten-year plan for increased cooperation with and aid for the Latin American countries. Widespread and worsening poverty, a literacy rate of only about 50 per cent, and a mushrooming birth rate were among the problems the Latin Americans had to cope with. The Alliance stressed self-help, linked with American aid.

Kennedy made clear that America's stake in helping its southern neighbors was in part to prove that economic progress was possible in a system of political freedom, and to counteract the lure of the Communist system newly adopted by Castro's Cuba. He explained what was at issue in a speech at the University of Costa Rica at San José, March 20, 1963, during a meeting of Central American presidents:

For the past three days the presidents of seven American nations have been grappling with the central question which faces this country, my own country, and our hemisphere, and that is whether, under a system of political liberty, we can solve the economic problems that press upon our people. We are embarked upon a great adventure together, and that is the task of demonstrating to a watching world that free men can conquer the ancient enemies of man, poverty, ignorance, and hunger; of protecting freedom against those who would destroy it; of bringing hope to those who search for hope; of extending liberty to those who lack it.

This is an immense task, filled with difficulty and hardship and danger, but you have been given an opportunity to shape the destiny of man which has been given to no other generation in the last 2,000 years. And as a fellow American, I know that you welcome that responsibility and that opportunity. What Franklin Roosevelt said to the American

124

people in the 1930's I say to you now: This generation of Americans, your generation of Americans, has a rendezvous with destiny. I am confident that you will meet that rendezvous. . . .

And if the task of progress with freedom is more complex, more subtle, and more difficult than the promise of progress without freedom, we are unafraid of that challenge. We are committed to four basic principles in this hemisphere in the Alliance for Progress. The first is the right of every nation to govern itself, to be free from outside dictation and coercion, to mold its own economy and society in any fashion consistent with the will of the people.

Second is the right of every individual citizen to political liberty, the right to speak his own views, to worship God in his own way, to select the government which rules him, and to reject it when it no longer serves the needs of a nation.

And third is the right to social justice, the right of every citizen to participate in the progress of his nation. This means land for the landless, and education for those who are denied their education today in this hemisphere. It means that ancient institutions which perpetuate privilege must give way. It means that rich and poor alike must bear the burden and the opportunity of building a nation. It will not be easy to achieve social justice, but freedom cannot last without it.

And the fourth principle of the Alliance is the right of every nation to make economic progress with modern technological means. This is the job, it seems to me, of all of us in this hemisphere in this decade, to demonstrate that we can provide a better life for our people under a system of freedom, to demonstrate that it is our adversaries who must build walls to hold their people in, who must deny their people the right not only to freedom, but economic advancement as well.

125

The continuing struggle to maintain peace was, as always, a major concern of the President and of the American people. There is no simple military solution to the cold war, and no assurance of a stable peace. Unending vigilance to prevent escalation of hostilities into a war that could destroy the world while remaining firm in defense of liberty was the hardest—and only possible—course to follow. The President discussed the never-ending effort on October 19, 1963, at the University of Maine:

I speak on the need for a more exact understanding of the true correlation of forces in the conduct of foreign affairs.

One year ago this coming week, the United States and the world were gripped with a somber prospect of a military confrontation between the two great nuclear powers [over Russia's Cuban missile bases]. The American people have good reason to recall with pride their conduct throughout that harrowing week. For they neither dissolved in panic nor rushed headlong into reckless belligerence. Well aware of the risks of resistance, they nevertheless refused to tolerate the Soviets' attempt to place nuclear weapons in this hemisphere, but recognized at the same time that our preparation for the use of force necessarily required a simultaneous search for fair and peaceful solutions.

The extraordinary events of that week and the weeks that followed are now history—a history which is differently interpreted, differently recounted, and differently labeled among various observers and nations. Some hail it as the West's greatest victory, others as a bitter defeat. Some mark it as a turning point in the cold war, others as proof of its permanence. Some attribute the Soviet withdrawal of missiles to our military actions alone, while some credit solely our use of negotiations. Some view the entire episode as an example of Communist duplicity, while some others abroad

126

have accepted the assertion that it indicated the Soviets' peaceful intentions.

While only the passage of time and events can reveal in full the true perspective of last October's drama, it is already clear that no single, simple view of this kind can be wholly accurate in this case. While both caution and common sense proscribe our boasting of it in the traditional terms of unconditional military victory, only the most zealous partisan can attempt to call it a defeat. While it is too late to say that nothing is changed in Soviet-American relations, it is too early to assume that the change is permanent. There are new rays of hope on the horizon, but we still live in the shadows of war.

Let us examine the events of twelve months ago, therefore, and the events of the past twelve months, and the events of the next twelve months, in the context of calm and caution. It is clear there will be further disagreement between ourselves and the Soviets as well as further agreements. There will be setbacks in our nation's endeavors on behalf of freedom as well as successes. For a pause in the cold war is not a lasting peace—and a *détente* does not equal disarmament. The United States must continue to seek a relaxation of tensions, but we have no cause to relax our vigilance.

A year ago it would have been easy to assume that all-out war was inevitable, that any agreement with the Soviets was impossible, and that an unlimited arms race was unavoidable. Today it is equally easy for some to assume that the cold war is over, that all outstanding issues between the Soviets and ourselves can be quickly and satisfactorily settled, and that we shall now have, in the words of the Psalmist, an "abundance of peace so long as the moon endureth."

The fact of the matter is, of course, that neither view is correct. We have, it is true, made some progress on a long

127

journey. We have achieved new opportunities which we cannot afford to waste. We have concluded with the Soviets a few limited, enforceable agreements or arrangements of mutual benefit to both sides and to the world.

But a change in atmosphere and in emphasis is not a reversal of purpose. Mr. Khrushchev himself has said that there can be no coexistence in the field of ideology. In addition, there are still major areas of tension and conflict, from Berlin to Cuba to Southeast Asia. The United States and the Soviet Union still have wholly different concepts of the world, its freedom, its future. We still have wholly different views on the so-called wars of liberation and the use of subversion. And so long as these basic differences continue, they cannot and should not be concealed. They set limits to the possibilities of agreements, and they will give rise to further crises, large and small, in the months and years ahead, both in the areas of direct confrontation—Germany and the Caribbean—and in areas where events beyond our control could involve us both—areas such as Africa and Asia and the Middle East.

In times such as these, therefore, there is nothing inconsistent with signing an atmospheric nuclear test ban, on the one hand, and testing underground on the other; about being willing to sell to the Soviets our surplus wheat while refusing to sell strategic items; about probing their interest in a joint lunar landing while making a major effort to master this new environment; or about exploring the possibilities of disarmament while maintaining our stockpile of arms. For all of these moves, and all of these elements of American policy and allied policy toward the Soviet Union, are directed at a single, comprehensive goal—namely, convincing the Soviet leaders that it is dangerous for them to engage in direct or indirect aggression, futile for them to attempt to impose their will and their system on other unwilling people, and beneficial to them, as well as to the world, to join in the achievement of a genuine and enforceable peace.

While the road to that peace is long and hard, and full of traps and pitfalls, there is no reason not to take each step that we can safely take. It is in our national self-interest to ban nuclear testing in the atmosphere so that all of our citizens can breathe more easily. It is in our national self-interest to sell surplus wheat in storage to feed Russians and Eastern Europeans who are willing to divert large portions of their limited foreign exchange reserves away from the implements of war. It is in our national self-interest to keep weapons of mass destruction out of outer space; to maintain an emergency communications link with Moscow, and to substitute joint and peaceful exploration in the Antarctic and outer space for cold war exploitation.

No one of these small advances, nor all of them together, can be interpreted as meaning that the Soviets are abandoning their basic aims and ambitions. Nor should any future, less friendly Soviet action—whether it is a stoppage on the autobahn, or a veto in the U.N., or a spy in our midst, or new trouble elsewhere—cause us to regret the steps we have taken. Even if those steps themselves should be undone by the violation or renunciation of the test-ban treaty, for example, or by a decision to decline American wheat, there would still be no reason to regret the fact that this nation has made every responsible effort to improve relations.

For without our making such an effort, we could not maintain the leadership and respect of the free world. Without our making such an effort, we could not convince our adversaries that war was not in their interest. And without our making such an effort, we could never, in case of war, satisfy our own hearts and minds that we had done all that could be done to avoid the holocaust of endless death and destruction.

Historians report that in 1914, with most of the world already plunged in war, Prince Bülow, the former German Chancellor, said to the then Chancellor Bethmann-Hollweg: "How did it all happen?" And Bethmann-Hollweg replied: "Ah, if only one knew." If this planet is ever ravaged by nuclear war, if 300 million Americans, Russians, and Europeans are wiped out by a sixty-minute nuclear exchange, if the survivors of that devastation can then endure the fire, poison, chaos, and catastrophe, I do not want one of those survivors to ask another, "How did it all happen?" and to receive the incredible reply, "Ah, if only one knew."

Therefore, while maintaining our readiness for war, let us exhaust every avenue for peace. Let us always make clear our willingness to talk, if talk will help, and our readiness to fight, if fight we must. Let us resolve to be the masters, not the victims, of our history, controlling our own destiny without giving way to blind suspicion and emotion. Let us distinguish between our hopes and our illusions, always hoping for steady progress toward less critically dangerous relations with the Soviets, but never laboring under any illusions about Communist methods or Communist goals.

Let us recognize both the gains we have made down the road to peace and the great distance yet to be covered. Let us not waste the present pause by either a needless renewal of tensions or a needless relaxation of vigilance. And let us recognize that we have made these gains and achieved this pause by the firmness we displayed a year ago as well as our restraint—by our efforts for defense as well as our efforts for peace.

In short, when we think of peace in this country, let us think of both our capacity to deter aggression and our goal

130

of true disarmament. Let us think of both the strength of our Western alliances and the areas of East-West cooperation.

For the American eagle on the Presidential seal holds in his talons both the olive branch of peace and the arrows of military might. On the ceiling in the Presidential office, constructed many years ago, that eagle is facing the arrows of war on its left. But on the newer carpet on the floor, reflecting a change initiated by President Roosevelt and implemented by President Truman immediately after the war, that eagle is now facing the olive branch of peace. And it is that spirit, the spirit of both preparedness and peace, that this nation today is stronger than ever before—strengthened by both the increased power of our defenses and our increased efforts for peace—strengthened by both our resolve to resist coercion and our constant search for solutions. And it is in this spirit, I can assure you, that the American eagle still faces toward the olive branch of peace. In the months and years ahead, we intend to build both kinds of strength, during times of *détente* as well as tension, during periods of conflict as well as cooperation—until the world we pass on to our children is truly safe for diversity and freedom and the rule of law covers all.

A few months previously, on June 10, 1963, the President had defined the possibilities of peace at a commencement speech at American University in Washington, D.C. In this speech he announced a high-level meeting to discuss a nuclear test-ban treaty. That historic treaty, signed the next month by Russia, the United States, Great Britain, and about 100 other nations, prohibited atomic testing in the atmosphere, outer space, and under water, but not underground. The President also mentioned the possibility of service in a "National Service Corps." The organization was subsequently founded as VISTA, Volunteers in Service to America.

131

"There are few earthly things more beautiful than a university," wrote John Masefield, in his tribute to English universities—and his words are equally true today. He did not refer to spires and towers, to campus greens and ivied walls. He admired the splendid beauty of the university, he said, because it was "a place where those who hate ignorance may strive to know, where those who perceive truth may strive to make others see."

I have, therefore, chosen this time and this place to discuss a topic on which ignorance too often abounds and the truth is too rarely perceived—yet it is the most important topic on earth: world peace.

What kind of peace do I mean? What kind of peace do we seek? Not a Pax Americana enforced on the world by American weapons of war. Not the peace of the grave or the security of the slave. I am talking about genuine peace, the kind of peace that makes life on earth worth living, the kind that enables men and nations to grow and to hope and to build a better life for their children—not merely peace for Americans but peace for all men and women—not merely peace in our time but peace for all time.

I speak of peace because of the new face of war. Total war makes no sense in an age where great powers can maintain large and relatively invulnerable nuclear forces and refuse to surrender without resort to those forces. It makes no sense in an age when a single nuclear weapon contains almost ten times the explosive force delivered by all of the allied air forces in the Second World War. It makes no sense in an age when the deadly poisons produced by a nuclear exchange would be carried by wind and water and soil and seed to the far corners of the globe and to generations yet unborn.

Today the expenditure of billions of dollars every year on weapons acquired for the purpose of making sure we never need to use them is essential to keeping the peace. But surely the acquisition of such idle stockpiles—which can only destroy and never create—is not the only, much less the most efficient, means of assuring peace.

I speak of peace, therefore, as the necessary rational end of rational men. I realize that the pursuit of peace is not as dramatic as the pursuit of war—and frequently the words of the pursuer fall on deaf ears. But we have no more urgent task.

Some say that it is useless to speak of world peace or world law or world disarmament—and that it will be useless until the leaders of the Soviet Union adopt a more enlightened attitude. I hope they do. I believe we can help them do it. But I also believe that we must re-examine our own attitude—as individuals and as a nation—for our attitude is as essential as theirs. And every thoughtful citizen who despairs of war and wishes to bring peace should begin by looking inward—by examining his own attitude toward the possibilities of peace, toward the Soviet Union, toward the course of the cold war, and toward freedom and peace here at home.

First: Let us examine our attitude toward peace itself. Too many of us think it is impossible. Too many think it unreal. But that is a dangerous, defeatist belief. It leads to the conclusion that war is inevitable—that mankind is doomed—that we are gripped by forces we cannot control.

We need not accept that view. Our problems are man-made—therefore, they can be solved by man. And man can be as big as he wants. No problem of human destiny is beyond human beings. Man's reason and spirit have often solved the seemingly unsolvable—and we believe they can do it again.

I am not referring to the absolute, infinite concept of universal peace and good will of which some fantasies and fanatics dream. I do not deny the value of hopes and

133

dreams, but we merely invite discouragement and incredulity by making that our only and immediate goal.

Let us focus instead on a more practical, more attainable peace—based not on a sudden revolution in human nature but on a gradual evolution in human institutions—on a series of concrete actions and effective agreements which are in the interest of all concerned. There is no single, simple key to this peace—no grand or magic formula to be adopted by one or two powers. Genuine peace must be the product of many nations, the sum of many acts. It must be dynamic, not static, changing to meet the challenge of each new generation. For peace is a process—a way of solving problems.

With such a peace, there will be quarrels and conflicting interests, as there are within families and nations. World peace, like community peace, does not require that each man love his neighbor—it requires only that they live together in mutual tolerance, submitting their disputes to a just and peaceful settlement. And history teaches us that enmities between nations, as between individuals, do not last forever. However fixed our likes and dislikes may seem, the tide of time and events will often bring surprising changes in the relations between nations and neighbors.

So let us persevere. Peace need not be impracticable, and war need not be inevitable. By defining our goal more clearly, by making it seem more manageable and less remote, we can help all peoples to see it, to draw hope from it, and to move irresistibly toward it.

Second: Let us re-examine our attitude toward the Soviet Union. It is discouraging to think that their leaders may actually believe what their propagandists write. It is discouraging to read a recent authoritative Soviet text, *Military Strategy*, and find, on page after page, wholly baseless and incredible claims—such as the allegation that "American imperialist circles are preparing to unleash different types

134

of wars . . . that there is a very real threat of a preventive war being unleashed by American imperialists against the Soviet Union . . . [and that] the political aims of the American imperialists are to enslave economically and politically the European and other capitalist countries . . . [and] to achieve world domination . . . by means of aggressive wars." Truly, as it was written long ago: "The wicked flee when no man pursueth." Yet it is sad to read these Soviet statements—to realize the extent of the gulf between us. But it is also a warning—a warning to the American people not to fall into the same trap as the Soviets, not to see only a distorted and desperate view of the other side, not to see conflict as inevitable, accommodation as impossible, and communication as nothing more than an exchange of threats.

No government or social system is so evil that its people must be considered as lacking in virtue. As Americans, we find Communism profoundly repugnant as a negation of personal freedom and dignity. But we can still hail the Russian people for their many achievements—in science and space, in economic and industrial growth, in culture and in acts of courage.

Among the many traits the peoples of our two countries have in common, none is stronger than our mutual abhorrence of war. Almost unique among the major world powers, we have never been at war with each other. And no nation in the history of battle ever suffered more than the Soviet Union suffered in the course of the Second World War. At least 20 million lost their lives. Countless millions of homes and farms were burned or sacked. A third of the nation's territory, including nearly two thirds of its industrial base, was turned into a wasteland—a loss equivalent to the devastation of this country east of Chicago.

Today, should total war ever break out again—no matter

135

how—our two countries would become the primary targets. It is an ironic but accurate fact that the two strongest powers are the two in the most danger of devastation. All we have built, all we have worked for, would be destroyed in the first twenty-four hours. And even in the cold war, which brings burdens and dangers to so many countries, including this nation's closest allies—our two countries bear the heaviest burdens. For we are both devoting massive sums of money to weapons that could be better devoted to combating ignorance, poverty, and disease. We are both caught up in a vicious and dangerous cycle in which suspicion on one side breeds suspicion on the other, and new weapons beget counterweapons.

In short, both the United States and its allies, and the Soviet Union and its allies, have a mutually deep interest in a just and genuine peace and in halting the arms race. Agreements to this end are in the interests of the Soviet Union as well as ours—and even the most hostile nations can be relied upon to accept and keep those treaty obligations, and only those treaty obligations, which are in their own interest. So, let us not be blind to our differences, but let us also direct attention to our common interests and to the means by which those differences can be resolved. And if we cannot end now our differences, at least we can help make the world safe for diversity. For, in the final analysis, our most basic common link is that we all inhabit this small planet. We all breathe the same air. We all cherish our children's future. And we are all mortal.

Third: Let us re-examine our attitude toward the cold war, remembering that we are not engaged in debate, seeking to pile up debating points. We are not here distributing blame or pointing the finger of judgment. We must deal with the world as it is, and not as it might have been had the history of the last eighteen years been different.

136

We must, therefore, persevere in the search for peace in the hope that constructive changes within the Communist bloc might bring within reach solutions which now seem beyond us. We must conduct our affairs in such a way that it becomes in the Communists' interest to agree on a genuine peace. Above all, while defending our own vital interests, nuclear powers must avert those confrontations which bring an adversary to a choice of either a humiliating retreat or a nuclear war. To adopt that kind of course in the nuclear age would be evidence only of the bankruptcy of our policy—or of a collective death-wish for the world.

To secure these ends, America's weapons are nonprovocative, carefully controlled, designed to deter, and capable of selective use. Our military forces are committed to peace and disciplined in self-restraint. Our diplomats are instructed to avoid unnecessary irritants and purely rhetorical hostility.

For we can seek a relaxation of tensions without relaxing our guard. And, for our part, we do not need to use threats to prove that we are resolute. We do not need to jam foreign broadcasts out of fear our faith will be eroded. We are unwilling to impose our system on any unwilling people —but we are willing and able to engage in peaceful competition with any people on earth.

Meanwhile, we seek to strengthen the United Nations, to help solve its financial problems, to make it a more effective instrument for peace, to develop it into a genuine world security system—a system capable of resolving disputes on the basis of law, of insuring the security of the large and the small, and of creating conditions under which arms can finally be abolished.

At the same time we seek to keep peace inside the non-Communist world, where many nations, all of them our friends, are divided over issues which weaken Western unity, which invite Communist intervention, or which threaten to erupt into war. Our efforts in West New Guinea, in the Congo, in the Middle East, and in the Indian subcontinent have been persistent and patient despite criticism from both sides. We have also tried to set an example for others—by seeking to adjust small but significant differences with our own closest neighbors in Mexico and in Canada.

Speaking of other nations, I wish to make one point clear. We are bound to many nations by alliances. Those alliances exist because our concern and theirs substantially overlap. Our commitment to defend Western Europe and West Berlin, for example, stands undiminished because of the identity of our vital interests. The United States will make no deal with the Soviet Union at the expense of other nations and other peoples, not merely because they are our partners, but also because their interests and ours converge. Our interests converge, however, not only in defending the frontiers of freedom, but in pursuing the paths of peace. It is our hope—and the purpose of allied policies—to convince the Soviet Union that she, too, should let each nation choose its own future, so long as that choice does not interfere with the choices of others. The Communist drive to impose their political and economic system on others is the primary cause of world tension today. For there can be no doubt that, if all nations could refrain from interfering in the self-determination of others, the peace would be much more assured.

This will require a new effort to achieve world law—a new context for world discussions. It will require increased understanding between the Soviets and ourselves. And increased understanding will require increased contact and communication. One step in this direction is the proposed arrangement for a direct line between Moscow and Washington, to avoid on each side the dangerous delays, misunderstandings, and misreadings of the other's actions which might occur at a time of crisis.

We have also been talking in Geneva about other first-step measures of arms control, designed to limit the intensity of the arms race and to reduce the risks of accidental war. Our primary long-range interest in Geneva, however, is general and complete disarmament—designed to take place by stages, permitting parallel political developments to build the new institutions of peace which would take the place of arms. The pursuit of disarmament has been an effort of this government since the 1920's. It has been urgently sought by the past three administrations. And however dim the prospects may be today, we intend to continue this effort—to continue it in order that all countries, including our own, can better grasp what the problems and possibilities of disarmament are.

The one major area of these negotiations where the end is in sight, yet where a fresh start is badly needed, is in a treaty to outlaw nuclear tests. The conclusion of such a treaty, so near and yet so far, would check the spiraling arms race in one of its most dangerous areas. It would place the nuclear powers in a position to deal more effectively with one of the greatest hazards which man faces in 1963, the further spread of nuclear arms. It would increase our security—it would decrease the prospects of war. Surely this goal is sufficiently important to require our steady pursuit, yielding neither to the temptation to give up the whole effort nor the temptation to give up our insistence on vital and responsible safeguards.

I am taking this opportunity, therefore, to announce two important decisions in this regard.

First: Chairman Khrushchev, Prime Minister Macmillan, and I have agreed that high-level discussions will shortly begin in Moscow looking toward early agreement on a comprehensive test-ban treaty. Our hopes must be tempered with the caution of history—but with our hopes go the hopes of all mankind.

Second: To make clear our good faith and solemn convictions on the matter, I now declare that the United States does not propose to conduct nuclear tests in the atmosphere so long as other states do not do so. We will not be the first to resume. Such a declaration is no substitute for a formal binding treaty, but I hope it will help us achieve one. Nor would such a treaty be a substitute for disarmament, but I hope it will help us achieve it.

Finally, my fellow Americans, let us examine our attitude toward peace and freedom here at home. The quality and spirit of our own society must justify and support our efforts abroad. We must show it in the dedication of our own lives —as many of you will have a unique opportunity to do, by serving without pay in the Peace Corps abroad or in the proposed National Service Corps here at home.

But wherever we are, we must all, in our daily lives, live up to the age-old faith that peace and freedom walk together. In too many of our cities today, the peace is not secure because freedom is incomplete.

It is the responsibility of the executive branch at all levels of government—local, state, and national—to provide and protect that freedom for all of our citizens by all means within their authority. It is the responsibility of the legislative branch at all levels, wherever that authority is not now adequate, to make it adequate. And it is the responsibility of all citizens in all sections of this country to respect the rights of all others and to respect the law of the land.

All this is not unrelated to world peace. "When a man's ways please the Lord," the Scriptures tell us, "he maketh even his enemies to be at peace with him." And is not peace, in the last analysis, basically a matter of human rights—the right to live out our lives without fear of devastation—the right to breathe air as nature provided it—the right of future generations to a healthy existence?

While we proceed to safeguard our national interests, let us also safeguard human interests. And the elimination of war and arms is clearly in the interest of both. No treaty, however much it may be to the advantage of all, however tightly it may be worded, can provide absolute security against the risks of deception and evasion. But it can—if it is sufficiently in the interests of its signers—offer far more security and far fewer risks than an unabated, uncontrolled, unpredictable arms race.

The United States, as the world knows, will never start a war. We do not want a war. We do not now expect a war. This generation of Americans has already had enough—more than enough—of war and hate and oppression. We shall be prepared if others wish it. We shall be alert to try to stop it. But we shall also do our part to build a world of peace where the weak are safe and the strong are just. We are not helpless before that task or hopeless of its success. Confident and unafraid, we labor on—not toward a strategy of annihilation but toward a strategy of peace.

The need for enlightened leadership amid the complexity of world affairs, and for Americans to understand the nation's strength and purpose, was a basic concern to President Kennedy. He had prepared a speech to elucidate our position in the world, to be delivered at the Trade Mart in Dallas, Texas, Before he could deliver it, he was assassinated—on November 22, 1963.

The link between leadership and learning is indispensable in world affairs. Ignorance and misinformation can handicap the progress of a city or a company, but they can, if

141

allowed to prevail in foreign policy, handicap this country's security. In a world of complex and continuing problems, in a world full of frustrations and irritations, America's leadership must be guided by the lights of learning and reason—or else those who confuse rhetoric with reality and the plausible with the possible will gain the popular ascendancy with their seemingly swift and simple solutions to every world problem.

There will always be dissident voices heard in the land, expressing opposition without alternatives, finding fault but never favor, perceiving gloom on every side and seeking influence without responsibility. Those voices are inevitable.

But today other voices are heard in the land—voices preaching doctrines wholly unrelated to reality, wholly unsuited to the sixties, doctrines which apparently assume that words will suffice without weapons, that vituperation is as good as victory and that peace is a sign of weakness. At a time when the national debt is steadily being reduced in terms of its burden on our economy, they see that debt as the greatest single threat to our security. At a time when we are steadily reducing the number of Federal employees serving every thousand citizens, they fear those supposed hordes of civil servants far more than the actual hordes of opposing armies.

We cannot expect that everyone, to use the phrase of a decade ago, will "talk sense to the American people." But we can hope that fewer people will listen to nonsense. And the notion that this nation is headed for defeat through deficit, or that strength is but a matter of slogans, is nothing but just plain nonsense.

I want to discuss with you today the status of our strength and our security because this question clearly calls for the most responsible qualities of leadership and the most enlightened products of scholarship. For this nation's strength and security are not easily or cheaply obtained, nor are they quickly and simply explained. There are many kinds of strength and no one kind will suffice. Overwhelming nuclear strength cannot stop a guerrilla war. Formal pacts of alliance cannot stop internal subversion. Displays of material wealth cannot stop the disillusionment of diplomats subjected to discrimination.

Above all, words alone are not enough. The United States is a peaceful nation. And where our strength and determination are clear, our words need merely to convey conviction, not belligerence. If we are strong, our strength will speak for itself. If we are weak, words will be of no help.

I realize that this nation often tends to identify turning points in world affairs with the major addresses which preceded them. But it was not the Monroe Doctrine that kept all Europe away from this hemisphere—it was the strength of the British fleet and the width of the Atlantic Ocean. It was not General Marshall's speech at Harvard which kept Communism out of Western Europe—it was the strength and stability made possible by our military and economic assistance.

In this administration also it has been necessary at times to issue specific warnings—warnings that we could not stand by and watch the Communists conquer Laos by force, or intervene in the Congo, or swallow West Berlin, or maintain offensive missiles on Cuba. But while our goals were at least temporarily obtained in these and other instances, our successful defense of freedom was due not to the words we used, but to the strength we stood ready to use on behalf of the principles we stand ready to defend.

This strength is composed of many different elements,

ranging from the most massive deterrents to the most subtle influences. And all types of strength are needed—no one kind could do the job alone. . . .

America today is stronger than ever before. Our adversaries have not abandoned their ambitions, our dangers have not diminished, our vigilance cannot be relaxed. But now we have the military, the scientific, and the economic strength to do whatever must be done for the preservation and promotion of freedom.

That strength will never be used in pursuit of aggressive ambitions—it will always be used in pursuit of peace. It will never be used to promote provocations—it will always be used to promote the peaceful settlement of disputes.

We in this country, in this generation, are—by destiny rather than choice—the watchmen on the walls of world freedom. We ask, therefore, that we may be worthy of our power and responsibility, that we may exercise our strength with wisdom and restraint, and that we may achieve in our time and for all time the ancient vision of "peace on earth, good will toward men." That must always be our goal, and the righteousness of our cause must always underlie our strength. For as was written long ago: "Except the Lord keep the city, the watchman waketh but in vain."